Limberham by John Dry ___

or, The Kind Keeper

A COMEDY.

John Dryden was born on August 9th, 1631 in the village rectory of Aldwincle near Thrapston in Northamptonshire. As a boy Dryden lived in the nearby village of Titchmarsh, Northamptonshire. In 1644 he was sent to Westminster School as a King's Scholar.

Dryden obtained his BA in 1654, graduating top of the list for Trinity College, Cambridge that year.

Returning to London during The Protectorate, Dryden now obtained work with Cromwell's Secretary of State, John Thurloe.

At Cromwell's funeral on 23 November 1658 Dryden was in the company of the Puritan poets John Milton and Andrew Marvell. The setting was to be a sea change in English history. From Republic to Monarchy and from one set of lauded poets to what would soon become the Age of Dryden.

The start began later that year when Dryden published the first of his great poems, Heroic Stanzas (1658), a eulogy on Cromwell's death.

With the Restoration of the Monarchy in 1660 Dryden celebrated in verse with Astraea Redux, an authentic royalist panegyric.

With the re-opening of the theatres after the Puritan ban, Dryden began to also write plays. His first play, The Wild Gallant, appeared in 1663 but was not successful. From 1668 on he was contracted to produce three plays a year for the King's Company, in which he became a shareholder. During the 1660s and '70s, theatrical writing was his main source of income.

In 1667, he published Annus Mirabilis, a lengthy historical poem which described the English defeat of the Dutch naval fleet and the Great Fire of London in 1666. It established him as the pre-eminent poet of his generation, and was crucial in his attaining the posts of Poet Laureate (1668) and then historiographer royal (1670).

This was truly the Age of Dryden, he was the foremost English Literary figure in Poetry, Plays, translations and other forms.

In 1694 he began work on what would be his most ambitious and defining work as translator, The Works of Virgil (1697), which was published by subscription. It was a national event.

John Dryden died on May 12th, 1700, and was initially buried in St. Anne's cemetery in Soho, before being exhumed and reburied in Westminster Abbey ten days later.

Index of Contents

LIMBERHAM. AN INTRODUCTION

The extreme indelicacy of this play would, in the present times furnish ample and most just grounds for the unfavourable reception it met with from the public. But in the reign of Charles II. many plays were applauded, in which the painting is, at least, as coarse as that of Dryden. "Bellamira, or the Mistress," a gross translation by Sir Charles Sedley of Terence's "Eunuchus," had been often represented with the highest approbation. But the satire of Dryden was rather accounted too personal, than too loose. The character of Limberham has been supposed to represent Lauderdale, whose age and uncouth figure rendered ridiculous his ungainly affectation of fashionable vices. Mr Malone intimates a suspicion, that Shaftesbury was the person levelled at, whose lameness and infirmities made the satire equally poignant. In either supposition, a powerful and leading nobleman was offended, to whose party all seem to have drawn, whose loose conduct, in that loose age, exposed them to be duped like the hero of the play. It is a singular mark of the dissolute manners of those times, that an audience, to whom matrimonial infidelity was nightly held out, not only as the most venial of trespasses, but as a matter of triumphant applause, were unable to brook any ridicule, upon the mere transitory connection formed betwixt the keeper and his mistress. Dryden had spared neither kind of union; and accordingly his opponents exclaimed, "That he lampooned the court, to oblige his friends in the city, and ridiculed the city, to secure a promising lord at court; exposed the kind keepers of Covent Garden, to please the cuckolds of Cheapside; and drolled on the city Do-littles, to tickle the Covent-Garden Limberhams[1]."

Even Langbaine, relentless as he is in criticism, seems to have considered the condemnation of Limberham as the vengeance of the faction ridiculed.

"In this play, (which I take to be the best comedy of his) he so much exposed the keeping part of the town, that the play was stopt when it had but thrice appeared on the stage; but the author took a becoming care, that the things that offended on the stage, were either altered or omitted in the press. One of our modern writers, in a short satire against keeping, concludes thus:

"Dryden, good man, thought keepers to reclaim,
Writ a kind satire, call'd it Limberham.
This all the herd of letchers straight alarms;
From Charing-Cross to Bow was up in arms:
They damn'd the play all at one fatal blow,
And broke the glass, that did their picture show."

Mr Malone mentions his having seen a MS. copy of this play, found by Lord Bolingbroke among the sweepings of Pope's study, in which there occur several indecent passages, not to be found in the printed copy. These, doubtless, constituted the castrations, which, in obedience to the public voice, our author expunged from his play, after its condemnation. It is difficult to guess what could be the nature of the indecencies struck out, when we consider those which the poet deemed himself at liberty to retain.

The reader will probably easily excuse any remarks upon this comedy. It is not absolutely without humour, but is so disgustingly coarse, as entirely to destroy that merit. Langbaine, with his usual anxiety of research, traces back a few of the incidents to the novels of Cinthio Giraldi, and to those of some forgotten French authors.

Plays, even of this nature, being worth preservation, as containing genuine traces of the manners of the age in which they appear, I cannot but remark the promiscuous intercourse, which, in this comedy and others, is represented as taking place betwixt women of character, and those who made no pretensions to it. Bellamira in Sir Charles Sedley's play, and Mrs Tricksy in the following pages, are admitted into company with the modest female characters, without the least hint of exception or impropriety. Such were actually the manners of Charles the II.d's time, where we find the mistresses of the king, and his brothers, familiar in the highest circles. It appears, from the evidence in the case of the duchess of Norfolk for adultery, that Nell Gwyn was living with her Grace in familiar habits; her society, doubtless, paving the way for the intrigue, by which the unfortunate lady lost her rank and reputation[2]. It is always symptomatic of a total decay of morals, where female reputation neither confers dignity, nor excites pride, in its possessor; but is consistent with her mingling in the society of the libertine and the profligate.

Some of Dryden's libellers draw an invidious comparison betwixt his own private life and this satire; and exhort him to

Be to vices, which he practised, kind.

But of the injustice of this charge on Dryden's character, we have spoken fully elsewhere. Undoubtedly he had the licence of this, and his other dramatic writings, in his mind, when he wrote the following

verses; where the impurity of the stage is traced to its radical
source, the debauchery of the court:

Then courts of kings were held in high renown,
Ere made the common brothels of the town.
There virgins honourable vows received,
But chaste, as maids in monasteries, lived.
The king himself, to nuptial rites a slave,
No bad example to his poets gave;
And they, not bad, but in a vicious age,
Had not, to please the prince, debauched the stage.
Wife of Bath's Tale.

"Limberham" was acted at the Duke's Theatre in Dorset-Garden; for, being a satire upon a court vice, it
was deemed peculiarly calculated for that play-house. The concourse of the citizens thither is alluded to
in the prologue to "Marriage-a-la-Mode." Ravenscroft also, in his epilogue to the "Citizen turned
Gentleman," acted at the same theatre, disowns the patronage of the courtiers who kept mistresses,
probably because they Constituted the minor part of his audience:

From the court party we hope no success;
Our author is not one of the noblesse,
That bravely does maintain his miss in town,
Whilst my great lady is with speed sent down,
And forced in country mansion-house to fix.
That miss may rattle here in coach-and-six.

The stage for introducing "Limberham" was therefore judiciously chosen, although the piece was ill
received, and withdrawn after being only thrice represented. It was printed in 1678.

Footnotes

1. *Reasons for Mr Bayes changing his Religion, p. 24.*

2. *See State Trials, vol. viii. pp. 17, 18.*

TO THE RIGHT HONOURABLE JOHN, LORD VAUGHAN, &c[1].

MY LORD,

I cannot easily excuse the printing of a play at so unseasonable a time[2], when the great plot of the
nation, like one of Pharaoh's lean kine, has devoured its younger brethren of the stage. But however
weak my defence might be for this, I am sure I should not need any to the world for my dedication to
your lordship; and if you can pardon my presumption in it, that a bad poet should address himself to so
great a judge of wit, I may hope at least to escape with the excuse of Catullus, when he writ to Cicero:

Gratias tibi maximas Catullus
Agit, pessimus omnium, poeta;
Tanto pessimus omnium poeta,
Quanto tu optimns omnium patronus.

I have seen an epistle of Flecknoe's to a nobleman, who was by some extraordinary chance a scholar; (and you may please to take notice by the way, how natural the connection of thought is betwixt a bad poet and Flecknoe) where he begins thus: Quatuordecim jam elapsi sunt anni, &c.; his Latin, it seems, not holding out to the end of the sentence: but he endeavoured to tell his patron, betwixt two languages which he understood alike, that it was fourteen years since he had the happiness to know him. It is just so long, (and as happy be the omen of dulness to me, as it is to some clergymen and statesmen!) since your lordship has known, that there is a worse poet remaining in the world, than he of scandalous memory, who left it last[3]. I might enlarge upon the subject with my author, and assure you, that I have served as long for you, as one of the patriarchs did for his Old-Testament mistress; but I leave those flourishes, when occasion shall serve, for a greater orator to use, and dare only tell you, that I never passed any part of my life with greater satisfaction or improvement to myself, than those years which I have lived in the honour of your lordship's acquaintance; if I may have only the time abated when the public service called you to another part of the world, which, in imitation of our florid speakers, I might (if I durst presume upon the expression) call the parenthesis of my life.

That I have always honoured you, I suppose I need not tell you at this time of day; for you know I staid not to date my respects to you from that title which now you have, and to which you bring a greater addition by your merit, than you receive from it by the name; but I am proud to let others know, how long it is that I have been made happy by my knowledge of you; because I am sure it will give me a reputation with the present age, and with posterity. And now, my lord, I know you are afraid, lest I should take this occasion, which lies so fair for me, to acquaint the world with some of those excellencies which I have admired in you; but I have reasonably considered, that to acquaint the world, is a phrase of a malicious meaning; for it would imply, that the world were not already acquainted with them. You are so generally known to be above the meanness of my praises, that you have spared my evidence, and spoiled my compliment: Should I take for my common places, your knowledge both of the old and the new philosophy; should I add to these your skill in mathematics and history; and yet farther, your being conversant with all the ancient authors of the Greek and Latin tongues, as well as with the modern—I should tell nothing new to mankind; for when I have once but named you, the world will anticipate all my commendations, and go faster before me than I can follow. Be therefore secure, my lord, that your own fame has freed itself from the danger of a panegyric; and only give me leave to tell you, that I value the candour of your nature, and that one character of friendliness, and, if I may have leave to call it, kindness in you, before all those other which make you considerable in the nation[4].

Some few of our nobility are learned, and therefore I will not conclude an absolute contradiction in the terms of nobleman and scholar; but as the world goes now, 'tis very hard to predicate one upon the other; and 'tis yet more difficult to prove, that a nobleman can be a friend to poetry. Were it not for two or three instances in Whitehall, and in the town, the poets of this age would find so little encouragement for their labours, and so few understanders, that they might have leisure to turn pamphleteers, and augment the number of those abominable scribblers, who, in this time of licence, abuse the press, almost every day, with nonsense, and railing against the government.

It remains, my lord, that I should give you some account of this comedy, which you have never seen; because it was written and acted in your absence, at your government of Jamaica. It was intended for an honest satire against our crying sin of keeping; how it would have succeeded, I can but guess, for it was permitted to be acted only thrice. The crime, for which it suffered, was that which is objected against the satires of Juvenal, and the epigrams of Catullus, that it expressed too much of the vice which it decried. Your lordship knows what answer was returned by the elder of those poets, whom I last mentioned, to his accusers:

—castum esse decet pium poetam
Ipsum. Versiculos nihil necesse est:
Qui tum denique habent salem ac leporem
Si sint molliculi et parum pudici.

But I dare not make that apology for myself; and therefore have taken a becoming care, that those things which offended on the stage, might be either altered, or omitted in the press; for their authority is, and shall be, ever sacred to me, as much absent as present, and in all alterations of their fortune, who for those reasons have stopped its farther appearance on the theatre. And whatsoever hindrance it has been to me in point of profit, many of my friends can bear me witness, that I have not once murmured against that decree. The same fortune once happened to Moliere, on the occasion of his "Tartuffe;" which, notwithstanding, afterwards has seen the light, in a country more bigot than ours, and is accounted amongst the best pieces of that poet. I will be bold enough to say, that this comedy is of the first rank of those which I have written, and that posterity will be of my opinion. It has nothing of particular satire in it; for whatsoever may have been pretended by some critics in the town, I may safely and solemnly affirm, that no one character has been drawn from any single man; and that I have known so many of the same humour, in every folly which is here exposed, as may serve to warrant it from a particular reflection. It was printed in my absence from the town, this summer, much against my expectation; otherwise I had over-looked the press, and been yet more careful, that neither my friends should have had the least occasion of unkindness against me, nor my enemies of upbraiding me; but if it live to a second impression, I will faithfully perform what has been wanting in this. In the mean time, my lord, I recommend it to your protection, and beg I may keep still that place in your favour which I have hitherto enjoyed; and which I shall reckon as one of the greatest blessings which can befall,

My Lord,

Your Lordship's most obedient,
Faithful servant,
JOHN DRYDEN.

Footnotes

1. John, Lord Vaughan, was the eldest surviving son of Richard, Earl of Carbery, to which title he afterwards succeeded. He was a man of literature, and president of the Royal Society from 1686 to 1689. Dryden was distinguished by his patronage as far back as 1664, being fourteen years before the acting of this play. Lord Vaughan had thus the honour of discovering and admiring the poet's genius, before the public applause had fixed his fame; and, probably better deserved the panegyric here bestowed, than was Usual among Dryden's patrons. He wrote a recommendatory copy of verses, which are prefixed to "The Conquest of Granada." Mr Malone informs us, that this accomplished nobleman died at Chelsea, on 16th January, 1712-13.

2. The great popish plot, that scene of mystery and blood, broke out in August 1678.

3. Flecknoe was a Roman Catholic priest, very much addicted to scribbling verses. His name has been chiefly preserved by our author's satire of "Mack-Flecknoe;" in which he has depicted Shadwell, as the literary son and heir of this wretched poetaster. A few farther particulars concerning him may be found prefixed to that poem. Flecknoe, from this dedication, appears to have been just deceased. The particular passage referred to has not been discovered; even Langbaine had never seen it: but Mr Malone points out a letter of Flecknoe to the Cardinal Barberini, whereof the first sentence is in Latin, and the next in English. Our author, in an uncommon strain of self-depreciation, or rather to give a neat turn to his sentence, has avouched himself to be a worse poet than Flecknoe. But expressions of modesty in a dedication, like those of panegyric, are not to be understood literally. As in the latter, Dryden often strains a note beyond Ela, so, on the present occasion, he has certainly sounded the very base string of humility. Poor Flecknoe, indeed, seems to have become proverbial, as the worst of poets. The Earl of Dorset thus begins a satire on Edward Howard:

Those damned antipodes to common sense,
Those toils to Flecknoe, pr'ythee, tell me whence
Does all this mighty mass of dulness spring,
Which in such loads thou to the stage dost bring?

4. There is a very flat and prosaic imitation of this sentiment in the Duke of Buckingham's lines to Pope:

And yet so wondrous, so sublime a thing
As the great Iliad, scarce could make me sing;
Except I justly could at once commend
A good companion, and as firm a friend;
One moral, or a mere well-natured deed,
Does all desert in sciences exceed.

Thus prose may be humbled, as well as exalted; into poetry.

PROLOGUE

True wit has seen its best days long ago;
It ne'er looked up, since we were dipt in show;
When sense in doggrel rhimes and clouds was lost,
And dulness flourished at the actor's cost.
Nor stopt it here; when tragedy was done,
Satire and humour the same fate have run,
And comedy is sunk to trick and pun.
Now our machining lumber will not sell,
And you no longer care for heaven or hell;
What stuff will please you next, the Lord can tell.
Let them, who the rebellion first began
To wit, restore the monarch, if they can;
Our author dares not be the first bold man.

He, like the prudent citizen, takes care,
To keep for better marts his staple ware;
His toys are good enough for Sturbridge fair.
Tricks were the fashion; if it now be spent,
'Tis time enough at Easter, to invent;
No man will make up a new suit for Lent.
If now and then he takes a small pretence,
To forage for a little wit and sense,
Pray pardon him, he meant you no offence.
Next summer, Nostradamus tells, they say,
That all the critics shall be shipped away,
And not enow be left to damn a play.
To every sail beside, good heaven, be kind;
But drive away that swarm with such a wind,
That not one locust may be left behind!

DRAMATIS PERSONÆ

ALDO, an honest, good-natured, free-hearted old gentleman of the town.
WOODALL, his son, under a false name; bred abroad, and now returned from travel.
LIMBERHAM, a tame, foolish keeper, persuaded by what is last said to him, and changing next word.
BRAINSICK, a husband, who, being well conceited of himself, despises his wife: vehement and eloquent,
as he thinks; but indeed a talker of nonsense.
GERVASE, WOODALL'S man: formal, and apt to give good counsel.
GILES, WOODALL'S cast servant.

MRS SAINTLY, an hypocritical fanatic, landlady of the boarding-house.
MRS TRICKSY, a termagant kept mistress.
MRS PLEASANCE, supposed daughter to MRS SAINTLY: Spiteful and satirical; but secretly in love with
WOODALL.
MRS BRAINSICK.
JUDITH, a maid of the house.

SCENE—A Boarding-house in Town.

LIMBERHAM;

OR, THE KIND KEEPER.

ACT I

SCENE I—An open Garden-House; a table in it, and chairs.

Enter **WOODALL** and **GERVASE**.

WOODALL

Bid the footman receive the trunks and portmantua; and see them placed in the lodgings you have taken for me, while I walk a turn here in the garden.

GERVASE

It is already ordered, sir. But they are like to stay in the outer-room, till the mistress of the house return from morning exercise.

WOODALL

What, she's gone to the parish church, it seems, to her devotions!

GERVASE

No, sir; the servants have informed me, that she rises every morning, and goes to a private meeting-house; where they pray for the government, and practise against the authority of it.

WOODALL

And hast thou trepanned me into a tabernacle of the godly? Is this pious boarding-house a place for me, thou wicked varlet?

GERVASE

According to human appearance, I must confess, it is neither fit for you, nor you for it; but have patience, sir; matters are not so bad as they may seem. There are pious bawdy-houses in the world, or conventicles would not be so much frequented. Neither is it impossible, but a devout fanatic landlady of a boarding-house may be a bawd.

WOODALL

Ay, to those of her own church, I grant you, Gervase; but I am none of those.

GERVASE

If I were worthy to read you a lecture in the mystery of wickedness, I would instruct you first in the art of seeming holiness: But, heaven be thanked, you have a toward and pregnant genius to vice, and need not any man's instruction; and I am too good, I thank my stars, for the vile employment of a pimp.

WOODALL

Then thou art even too good for me; a worse man will serve my turn.

GERVASE

I call your conscience to witness, how often I have given you wholesome counsel; how often I have said to you, with tears in my eyes, master, or master Aldo—

WOODALL

Mr Woodall, you rogue! that is my nomme de guerre. You know I have laid by Aldo, for fear that name should bring me to the notice of my father.

GERVASE

Cry you mercy, good Mr Woodall. How often have I said,—Into what courses do you run! Your father sent you into France at twelve years old; bred you up at Paris, first in a college, and then at an academy: At the first, instead of running through a course of philosophy, you ran through all the bawdy-houses in town: At the latter, instead of managing the great horse, you exercised on your master's wife. What you did in Germany, I know not; but that you beat them all at their own weapon, drinking, and have brought home a goblet of plate from Munster, for the prize of swallowing a gallon of Rhenish more than the bishop.

WOODALL

Gervase, thou shalt be my chronicler; thou losest none of my heroic actions.

GERVASE

What a comfort are you like to prove to your good old father! You have run a campaigning among the French these last three years, without his leave; and now he sends for you back, to settle you in the world, and marry you to the heiress of a rich gentleman, of whom he had the guardianship, yet you do not make your application to him.

WOODALL

Pr'ythee, no more.

GERVASE

You are come over, have been in town above a week incognito, haunting play-houses, and other places, which for modesty I name not; and have changed your name from Aldo to Woodall, for fear of being discovered to him: You have not so much as inquired where he is lodged, though you know he is most commonly in London: And lastly, you have discharged my honest fellow-servant Giles, because—

WOODALL

Because he was too saucy, and was ever offering to give me counsel: Mark that, and tremble at his destiny.

GERVASE

I know the reason why I am kept; because you cannot be discovered by my means; for you took me up in France, and your father knows me not.

WOODALL

I must have a ramble in the town: When I have spent my money, I will grow dutiful, see my father, and ask for more. In the mean time, I have beheld a handsome woman at a play, I am fallen in love with her, and have found her easy: Thou, I thank thee, hast traced her to her lodging in this boarding-house, and hither I am come, to accomplish my design.

GERVASE

Well, heaven mend all. I hear our landlady's voice without;

[Noise.]

—and therefore shall defer my counsel to a fitter season.

WOODALL

Not a syllable of counsel: The next grave sentence, thou marchest after Giles. Woodall's my name; remember that.

[Enter **Mrs SAINTLY**.

Is this the lady of the house?

GERVASE
Yes, Mr Woodall, for want of a better, as she will tell you.

WOODALL
She has a notable smack with her! I believe zeal first taught the art of kissing close.

[Saluting her.

Mrs SAINTLY
You are welcome, gentleman. Woodall is your name?

WOODALL
I call myself so.

Mrs SAINTLY
You look like a sober discreet gentleman; there is grace in your countenance.

WOODALL
Some sprinklings of it, madam: We must not boast.

Mrs SAINTLY
Verily, boasting is of an evil principle.

WOODALL
Faith, madam—

Mrs SAINTLY
No swearing, I beseech you. Of what church are you?

WOODALL
Why, of Covent-Garden church, I think.

GERVASE
How lewdly and ignorantly he answers! [Aside] She means, of what religion are you?

WOODALL
O, does she so?—Why, I am of your religion, be it what it will; I warrant it a right one: I'll not stand with you for a trifle; presbyterian, independent, anabaptist, they are all of them too good for us, unless we had the grace to follow them.

Mrs SAINTLY

I see you are ignorant; but verily, you are a new vessel, and I may season you. I hope you do not use the parish-church.

WOODALL
Faith, madam—cry you mercy; (I forgot again) I have been in England but five days.

Mrs SAINTLY
I find a certain motion within me to this young man, and must secure him to myself, ere he see my lodgers. [Aside.]—O, seriously, I had forgotten; your trunk and portmantua are standing in the hall; your lodgings are ready, and your man may place them, if he please, while you and I confer together.

WOODALL
Go, Gervase, and do as you are directed.

[Exit **GERVASE**.

Mrs SAINTLY
In the first place, you must know, we are a company of ourselves, and expect you should live conformably and lovingly amongst us.

WOODALL
There you have hit me. I am the most loving soul, and shall be conformable to all of you.

Mrs SAINTLY
And to me especially. Then, I hope, you are no keeper of late hours.

WOODALL
No, no, my hours are very early; betwixt three and four in the morning, commonly.

Mrs SAINTLY
That must be amended; but, to remedy the inconvenience, I will myself sit up for you. I hope, you would not offer violence to me?

WOODALL
I think I should not, if I were sober.

Mrs SAINTLY
Then, if you were overtaken, and should offer violence, and I consent not, you may do your filthy part, and I am blameless.

WOODALL [Aside.]
I think the devil's in her; she has given me the hint again.—Well, it shall go hard, but I will offer violence sometimes; will that content you?

Mrs SAINTLY
I have a cup of cordial water in my closet, which will help to strengthen nature, and to carry off a debauch: I do not invite you thither; but the house will be safe a-bed, and scandal will be avoided.

WOODALL

Hang scandal; I am above it at those times.

Mrs SAINTLY

But scandal is the greatest part of the offence; you must be secret. And I must warn you of another thing; there are, besides myself, two more young women in my house.

WOODALL [Aside.]

That, besides herself, is a cooling card.—Pray, how young are they?

Mrs SAINTLY

About my age: some eighteen, or twenty, or thereabouts.

WOODALL

Oh, very good! Two more young women besides yourself, and both handsome?

Mrs SAINTLY

No, verily, they are painted outsides; you must not cast your eyes upon them, nor listen to their conversation: You are already chosen for a better work.

WOODALL

I warrant you, let me alone: I am chosen, I.

Mrs SAINTLY

They are a couple of alluring wanton minxes.

WOODALL

Are they very alluring, say you? very wanton?

Mrs SAINTLY

You appear exalted, when I mention those pit-falls of iniquity.

WOODALL

Who, I exalted? Good faith, I am as sober, a melancholy poor soul!—

Mrs SAINTLY

I see this abominable sin of swearing is rooted in you. Tear it out; oh, tear it out! it will destroy your precious soul.

WOODALL

I find we two shall scarce agree: I must not come to your closet when I have got a bottle; for, at such a time, I am horribly given to it.

Mrs SAINTLY

Verily, a little swearing may be then allowable: You may swear you love me, it is a lawful oath; but then, you must not look on harlots.

WOODALL

I must wheedle her, and whet my courage first on her; as a good musician always preludes before a tune. Come, here is my first oath.

[Embracing her.

[Enter **ALDO.**

ALDO
How now, Mrs Saintly! what work have we here towards?

WOODALL [Aside.]
Aldo, my own natural father, as I live! I remember the lines of that hide-bound face: Does he lodge here? If he should know me, I am ruined.

Mrs SAINTLY
Curse on his coming! he has disturbed us. [Aside.] Well, young gentleman, I shall take a time to instruct you better.

WOODALL
You shall find me an apt scholar.

Mrs SAINTLY
I must go abroad upon some business; but remember your promise, to carry yourself soberly, and without scandal in my family; and so I leave you to this gentleman, who is a member of it.

[Exit **Mrs SAINTLY.**

ALDO [Aside.]
Before George, a proper fellow, and a swinger he should be, by his make! the rogue would humble a whore, I warrant him.—You are welcome, sir, amongst us; most heartily welcome, as I may say.

WOODALL
All's well: he knows me not.—Sir, your civility is obliging to a stranger, and may befriend me, in the acquaintance of our fellow-lodgers.

ALDO
Hold you there, sir: I must first understand you a little better; and yet, methinks, you should be true to love.

WOODALL
Drinking and wenching are but slips of youth: I had those two good qualities from my father.

ALDO
Thou, boy! Aha, boy! a true Trojan, I warrant thee!

[Hugging him.]

Well, I say no more; but you are lighted into such a family, such food for concupiscence, such bona roba's!

WOODALL
One I know, indeed; a wife: But bona roba's, say you?

ALDO
I say, bona roba's, in the plural number.

WOODALL
Why, what a Turk Mahomet shall I be! No, I will not make myself drunk with the conceit of so much joy: The fortune's too great for mortal man; and I a poor unworthy sinner.

ALDO
Would I lie to my friend? Am I a man? Am I a christian? There is that wife you mentioned, a delicate little wheedling devil, with such an appearance of simplicity; and with that, she does so undermine, so fool her conceited husband, that he despises her!

WOODALL
Just ripe for horns: His destiny, like a Turk's, is written in his forehead.[1]

ALDO
Peace, peace! thou art yet ordained for greater things. There is another, too, a kept mistress, a brave strapping jade, a two-handed whore!

WOODALL
A kept mistress, too! my bowels yearn to her already: she is certain prize.

ALDO
But this lady is so termagant an empress! and he is so submissive, so tame, so led a keeper, and as proud of his slavery as a Frenchman. I am confident he dares not find her false, for fear of a quarrel with her; because he is sure to be at the charges of the war. She knows he cannot live without her, and therefore seeks occasions of falling out, to make him purchase peace. I believe she is now aiming at a settlement.

WOODALL
Might not I ask you one civil question? How pass you your time in this noble family? For I find you are a lover of the game, and I should be loth to hunt in your purlieus.

ALDO
I must first tell you something of my condition. I am here a friend to all of them; I am their factotum, do all their business; for, not to boast, sir, I am a man of general acquaintance: There is no news in town, either foreign or domestic, but I have it first; no mortgage of lands, no sale of houses, but I have a finger in them.

WOODALL
Then, I suppose, you are a gainer by your pains.

ALDO

No, I do all gratis, and am most commonly a loser; only a buck sometimes from this good lord, or that good lady in the country: and I eat it not alone, I must have company.

WOODALL
Pray, what company do you invite?

ALDO
Peace, peace, I am coming to you: Why, you must know I am tender-natured; and if any unhappy difference have arisen betwixt a mistress and her gallant, then I strike in, to do good offices betwixt them; and, at my own proper charges, conclude the quarrel with a reconciling supper.

WOODALL
I find the ladies of pleasure are beholden to you.

ALDO
Before George, I love the poor little devils. I am indeed a father to them, and so they call me: I give them my counsel, and assist them with my purse. I cannot see a pretty sinner hurried to prison by the land-pirates, but nature works, and I must bail her; or want a supper, but I have a couple of crammed chickens, a cream tart, and a bottle of wine to offer her.

WOODALL
Sure you expect some kindness in return.

ALDO
Faith, not much: Nature in me is at low water-mark; my body's a jade, and tires under me; yet I love to smuggle still in a corner; pat them down, and pur over them; but, after that, I can do them little harm.

WOODALL
Then I'm acquainted with your business: You would be a kind of deputy-fumbler under me.

ALDO
You have me right. Be you the lion, to devour the prey; I am your jackall, to provide it for you: There will be a bone for me to pick.

WOODALL
Your humility becomes your age. For my part, I am vigorous, and throw at all.

ALDO
As right as if I had begot thee! Wilt thou give me leave to call thee son?

WOODALL
With all my heart.

ALDO
Ha, mad son!

WOODALL
Mad daddy!

ALDO

Your man told me, you were just returned from travel: What parts have you last visited?

WOODALL

I came from France.

ALDO

Then, perhaps, you may have known an ungracious boy of mine there.

WOODALL

Like enough: Pray, what's his name?

ALDO

George Aldo.

WOODALL

I must confess I do know the gentleman; satisfy yourself, he's in health, and upon his return.

ALDO

That's some comfort: But, I hear, a very rogue, a lewd young fellow.

WOODALL

The worst I know of him is, that he loves a wench; and that good quality he has not stolen.

[Music at the Balcony over head: **Mrs TRICKSY** and **JUDITH** appear.]

—Hark! There's music above.

ALDO

'Tis at my daughter Tricksy's lodging; the kept mistress I told you of, the lass of mettle. But for all she carries it so high, I know her pedigree; her mother's a sempstress in Dog-and-Bitch yard, and was, in her youth, as right as she is.

WOODALL

Then she's a two-piled punk, a punk of two descents.

ALDO

And her father, the famous cobler, who taught Walsingham to the black-birds. How stand thy affections to her, thou lusty rogue?

WOODALL

All on fire: A most urging creature!

ALDO

Peace! they are beginning.

A SONG.

I.
'Gainst keepers we petition,
Who would inclose the common:
'Tis enough to raise sedition
In the free-born subject, woman.
Because for his gold,
I my body have sold,
He thinks I'm a slave for my life;
He rants, domineers,
He swaggers and swears,
And would keep me as bare as his wife.

II.
'Gainst keepers we petition, &c.
'Tis honest and fair,
That a feast I prepare;
But when his dull appetite's o'er,
I'll treat with the rest
Some welcomer guest,
For the reckoning was paid me before.

WOODALL
A song against keepers! this makes well for us lusty lovers.

Mrs TRICKSY [Above.]
Father, father Aldo!

ALDO
Daughter Tricksy, are you there, child? your friends at Barnet are all well, and your dear master Limberham, that noble Hephestion, is returning with them.

Mrs TRICKSY
And you are come upon the spur before, to acquaint me with the news.

ALDO
Well, thou art the happiest rogue in a kind keeper! He drank thy health five times, supernaculum,[2] to my son Brain-sick; and dipt my daughter Pleasance's little finger, to make it go down more glibly:[3] And, before George, I grew tory rory, as they say, and strained a brimmer through the lily-white smock, i'faith.

Mrs TRICKSY
You will never leave these fumbling tricks, father, till you are taken up on suspicion of manhood, and have a bastard laid at your door: I am sure you would own it, for your credit.

ALDO
Before George, I should not see it starve, for the mother's sake: For, if she were a punk, she was good-natured, I warrant her.

WOODALL [Aside.]
Well, if ever son was blest with a hopeful father, I am.

Mrs TRICKSY
Who is that gentleman with you?

ALDO
A young monsieur returned from travel; a lusty young rogue; a true-milled whoremaster, with the right stamp. He is a fellow-lodger, incorporate in our society: For whose sake he came hither, let him tell you.

WOODALL [Aside.]
Are you gloating already? then there's hopes, i'faith.

Mrs TRICKSY
You seem to know him, father.

ALDO
Know him! from his cradle—What's your name?

WOODALL
Woodall.

ALDO
Woodall of Woodall; I knew his father; we were contemporaries, and fellow-wenchers in our youth.

WOODALL [Aside.]
My honest father stumbles into truth, in spite of lying.

Mrs TRICKSY
I was just coming down to the garden-house, before you came.

[**Mrs TRICKSY** descends.

ALDO
I am sorry I cannot stay to present my son, Woodall, to you; but I have set you together, that's enough for me.

[Exit.

WOODALL [Alone.]
'Twas my study to avoid my father, and I have run full into his mouth: and yet I have a strong hank upon him too; for I am privy to as many of his virtues, as he is of mine. After all, if I had an ounce of discretion left, I should pursue this business no farther: but two fine women in a house! well, it is resolved, come what will on it, thou art answerable for all my sins, old Aldo—

[Enter **Mrs TRICKSY**, with a box of essences.

Here she comes, this heir-apparent of a sempstress, and a cobler! And yet, as she's adorned, she looks like any princess of the blood.

[Salutes her.

Mrs TRICKSY [Aside.]
What a difference there is between this gentleman, and my feeble keeper, Mr Limberham! he's to my wish, if he would but make the least advances to me.—Father Aldo tells me, sir, you are a traveller: What adventures have you had in foreign countries?

WOODALL
I have no adventures of my own, can deserve your curiosity; but, now I think on it, I can tell you one that happened to a French cavalier, a friend of mine, at Tripoli.

Mrs TRICKSY
No wars, I beseech you: I am so weary of father Aldo's Loraine and Crequi.

WOODALL
Then this is as you would desire it, a love-adventure. This French gentleman was made a slave to the Dey of Tripoli; by his good qualities, gained his master's favour; and after, by corrupting an eunuch, was brought into the seraglio privately, to see the Dey's mistress.

Mrs TRICKSY
This is somewhat; proceed, sweet sir.

WOODALL
He was so much amazed, when he first beheld her leaning over a balcony, that he scarcely dared to lift his eyes, or speak to her.

Mrs TRICKSY [Aside.]
I find him now.—But what followed of this dumb interview?

WOODALL
The nymph was gracious, and came down to him; but with so goddess-like a presence, that the poor gentleman was thunder-struck again.

Mrs TRICKSY
That savoured little of the monsieur's gallantry, especially when the lady gave him encouragement.

WOODALL
The gentleman was not so dull, but he understood the favour, and was presuming enough to try if she were mortal. He advanced with more assurance, and took her fair hands: was he not too bold, madam? and would not you have drawn back yours, had you been in the sultana's place?

Mrs TRICKSY
If the sultana liked him well enough to come down into the garden to him, I suppose she came not thither to gather nosegays.

WOODALL
Give me leave, madam, to thank you, in my friend's behalf, for your favourable judgment.

[Kisses her hand.]

He kissed her hand with an exceeding transport; and finding that she prest his at the same instant, he proceeded with a greater eagerness to her lips—but, madam, the story would be without life, unless you give me leave to act the circumstances.

[Kisses her.

Mrs TRICKSY
Well, I'll swear you are the most natural historian!

WOODALL
But now, madam, my heart beats with joy, when I come to tell you the sweetest part of his adventure: opportunity was favourable, and love was on his side; he told her, the chamber was more private, and a fitter scene for pleasure. Then, looking on her eyes, he found them languishing; he saw her cheeks blushing, and heard her voice faultering in a half-denial: he seized her hand with an amorous ecstacy, and—

[Takes her hand.

Mrs TRICKSY
Hold, sir, you act your part too far. Your friend was unconscionable, if he desired more favours at the first interview.

WOODALL
He both desired and obtained them, madam, and so will—

Mrs TRICKSY [A noise within.]
Heavens! I hear Mr Limberham's voice: he's returned from Barnet.

WOODALL
I'll avoid him.

Mrs TRICKSY
That's impossible; he'll meet you. Let me think a moment:—Mrs Saintly is abroad, and cannot discover you: have any of the servants seen you?

WOODALL
None.

Mrs TRICKSY
Then you shall pass for my Italian merchant of essences: here's a little box of them just ready.

WOODALL
But I speak no Italian; only a few broken scraps, which I picked from Scaramouch and Harlequin at Paris.

Mrs TRICKSY

You must venture that: When we are rid of Limberham, 'tis but slipping into your chamber, throwing off your black perriwig, and riding suit, and you come out an Englishman. No more; he's here.

[Enter **LIMBERHAM**.

LIMBERHAM

Why, how now, Pug? Nay, I must lay you over the lips, to take hansel of them, for my welcome.

Mrs TRICKSY [Putting him back.]
Foh! how you smell of sweat, dear!

LIMBERHAM

I have put myself into this same unsavoury heat, out of my violent affection to see thee, Pug. Before George, as father Aldo says, I could not live without thee; thou art the purest bed-fellow, though I say it, that I did nothing but dream of thee all night; and then I was so troublesome to father Aldo, (for you must know he and I were lodged together) that, in my conscience, I did so kiss him, and so hug him in my sleep!

Mrs TRICKSY

I dare be sworn 'twas in your sleep; for, when you are waking, you are the most honest, quiet bed-fellow, that ever lay by woman.

LIMBERHAM

Well, Pug, all shall be amended; I am come home on purpose to pay old debts. But who is that same fellow there? What makes he in our territories?

Mrs TRICKSY

You oaf you, do you not perceive it is the Italian seignior, who is come to sell me essences?

LIMBERHAM

Is this the seignior? I warrant you, it is he the lampoon was made on.

[Sings the tune of Seignior, and ends with, Ho, ho.

Mrs TRICKSY

Pr'ythee leave thy foppery, that we may have done with him. He asks an unreasonable price, and we cannot agree. Here, seignior, take your trinkets, and be gone.

WOODALL [Taking the box.]
A dio, seigniora.

LIMBERHAM

Hold, pray stay a little, seignior; a thing is come into my head of the sudden.

Mrs TRICKSY

What would you have, you eternal sot? the man's in haste.

LIMBERHAM

But why should you be in your frumps, Pug, when I design only to oblige you? I must present you with this box of essences; nothing can be too dear for thee.

Mrs TRICKSY

Pray let him go, he understands no English.

LIMBERHAM

Then how could you drive a bargain with him, Pug?

Mrs TRICKSY

Why, by signs, you coxcomb.

LIMBERHAM

Very good! then I'll first pull him by the sleeve, that's a sign to stay. Look you, Mr Seignior, I would make a present of your essences to this lady; for I find I cannot speak too plain to you, because you understand no English. Be not you refractory now, but take ready money: that's a rule.

WOODALL

Seignioro, non intendo Inglese.

LIMBERHAM

This is a very dull fellow! he says, he does not intend English. How much shall I offer him, Pug?

Mrs TRICKSY

If you will present me, I have bidden him ten guineas.

LIMBERHAM

And, before George, you bid him fair. Look you, Mr Seignior, I will give you all these. 1, 2, 3, 4, 5, 6, 7, 8, 9, and 10. Do you see, Seignior?

WOODALL

Seignior, si.

LIMBERHAM

Lo' you there, Pug, he does see. Here, will you take me at my word?

WOODALL [Shrugging up]

Troppo poco, troppo poco.

LIMBERHAM

A poco, a poco! why a pox on you too, an' you go to that. Stay, now I think on't, I can tickle him up with French; he'll understand that sure. Monsieur, voulez vous prendre ces dix guinees, pour ces essences? mon foy c'est assez.

WOODALL

Chi vala, amici: Ho di casa! taratapa, taratapa, eus, matou, meau!—[To her.] I am at the end of my Italian; what will become of me?

Mrs TRICKSY [To him.]
Speak any thing, and make it pass for Italian; but be sure you take his money.

WOODALL
Seignior, io non canno takare ten guinneo possibilmentè; 'tis
to my losso.

LIMBERHAM
That is, Pug, he cannot possibly take ten guineas, 'tis to his loss: Now I understand him; this is almost English.

Mrs TRICKSY
English! away, you fop: 'tis a kind of lingua Franca, as I have heard the merchants call it; a certain compound language, made up of all tongues, that passes through the Levant.

LIMBERHAM
This lingua, what you call it, is the most rarest language! I understand it as well as if it were English; you shall see me answer him: Seigniore, stay a littlo, and consider wello, ten guinnio is monyo, a very considerablo summo.

Mrs TRICKSY
Come, you shall make it twelve, and he shall take it for my sake.

LIMBERHAM
Then, Seignioro, for Pugsakio, addo two moro: je vous donne bon advise: prenez vitement: prenez me à mon mot.

WOODALL
Io losero multo; ma pergagnare il vestro costumo, datemi hansello.

LIMBERHAM
There is both hansello and guinnio; tako, tako, and so good-morrow.

Mrs TRICKSY
Good-morrow, seignior; I like your spirits very well; pray let me have all your essence you can spare.

LIMBERHAM
Come, Puggio, and let us retire in secreto, like lovers, into our chambro; for I grow impatiento—bon matin, monsieur, bon matin et bon jour.

[Exeunt **LIMBERHAM** and **Mrs TRICKSY**.

WOODALL
Well, get thee gone, 'squire Limberhamo, for the easiest fool I ever knew, next my naunt of fairies in the Alchemist[4]. I have escaped, thanks to my mistress's lingua França: I'll steal to my chamber, shift my

perriwig and clothes; and then, with the help of resty Gervase, concert the business of the next campaign. My father sticks in my stomach still; but I am resolved to be Woodall with him, and Aldo with the women.

[Exit.

ACT II

SCENE I

Enter **WOODALL** and **GERVASE**.

WOODALL
Hitherto, sweet Gervase, we have carried matters swimmingly. I have danced in a net before my father, almost check-mated the keeper, retired to my chamber undiscovered, shifted my habit, and am come out an absolute monsieur, to allure the ladies. How sits my chedreux?

GERVASE
O very finely! with the locks combed down, like a mermaid's on a sign-post. Well, you think now your father may live in the same house with you till doomsday, and never find you; or, when he has found you, he will be kind enough not to consider what a property you have made of him. My employment is at an end; you have got a better pimp, thanks to your filial reverence.

WOODALL
Pr'ythee, what should a man do with such a father, but use him thus? besides, he does journey-work under me; 'tis his humour to fumble, and my duty to provide for his old age.

GERVASE
Take my advice yet; down o' your marrow bones, and ask forgiveness; espouse the wife he has provided for you; lie by the side of a wholesome woman, and procreate your own progeny in the fear of heaven.

WOODALL
I have no vocation to it, Gervase: A man of sense is not made for marriage; 'tis a game, which none but dull plodding fellows can play at well; and 'tis as natural to them, as crimp is to a Dutchman.

GERVASE
Think on't, however, sir; debauchery is upon its last legs in England: Witty men began the fashion, and now the fops are got into it, 'tis time to leave it.

[Enter **ALDO**.

ALDO
Son Woodall, thou vigorous young rogue, I congratulate thy good fortune; thy man has told me the adventure of the Italian merchant.

WOODALL

Well, they are now retired together, like Rinaldo and Armida, to private dalliance; but we shall find a time to separate their loves, and strike in betwixt them, daddy. But I hear there's another lady in the house, my landlady's fair daughter; how came you to leave her out of your catalogue?

ALDO
She's pretty, I confess, but most damnably honest; have a care of her, I warn you, for she's prying and malicious.

WOODALL
A twang of the mother; but I love to graff on such a crab-tree; she may bear good fruit another year.

ALDO
No, no, avoid her; I warrant thee, young Alexander, I will provide thee more worlds to conquer.

GERVASE [Aside.]
My old master would fain pass for Philip of Macedon, when he is little better than Sir Pandarus of Troy.

WOODALL
If you get this keeper out of doors, father, and give me but an opportunity—

ALDO
Trust my diligence; I will smoke him out, as they do bees, but I will make him leave his honey-comb.

GERVASE[Aside.]
If I had a thousand sons, none of the race of the Gervases should ever be educated by thee, thou vile old Satan!

ALDO
Away, boy! Fix thy arms, and whet, like the lusty German boys, before a charge: He shall bolt immediately.

WOODALL
O, fear not the vigorous five-and-twenty.

ALDO
Hold, a word first: Thou saidst my son was shortly to come over.

WOODALL
So he told me.

ALDO
Thou art my bosom friend.

GERVASE [Aside.]
Of an hour's acquaintance.

ALDO

Be sure thou dost not discover my frailties to the young scoundrel: 'Twere enough to make the boy my master. I must keep up the dignity of old age with him.

WOODALL
Keep but your own counsel, father; for whatever he knows, must come from you.

ALDO
The truth on't is, I sent for him over; partly to have married him, and partly because his villainous bills came so thick upon me, that I grew weary of the charge.

GERVASE
He spared for nothing; he laid it on, sir, as I have heard.

WOODALL
Peace, you lying rogue!—Believe me, sir, bating his necessary expences of women, which I know you would not have him want, in all things else, he was the best manager of your allowance; and, though I say it—

GERVASE[Aside.]
That should not say it.

WOODALL
The most hopeful young gentleman in Paris.

ALDO
Report speaks otherwise; and, before George, I shall read him a wormwood lecture, when I see him. But, hark, I hear the door unlock; the lovers are coming out: I'll stay here, to wheedle him abroad; but you must vanish.

WOODALL
Like night and the moon, in the Maid's Tragedy: I into mist; you into day[5].

[Exeunt **WOODALL**. and **GERVASE**.

SCENE Changes to Limberham's Apartment

Enter **LIMBERHAM** and **Mrs TRICKSY.**

LIMBERHAM
Nay, but dear sweet honey Pug, forgive me but this once: It may be any man's case, when his desires are too vehement.

Mrs TRICKSY
Let me alone; I care not.

LIMBERHAM

But then thou wilt not love me, Pug.

ALDO
How now, son Limberham? There's no quarrel towards, I hope.

Mrs TRICKSY
You had best tell now, and make yourself ridiculous.

LIMBERHAM
She's in passion: Pray do you moderate this matter, father Aldo.

Mrs TRICKSY
Father Aldo! I wonder you are not ashamed to call him so; you may be his father, if the truth were known.

ALDO
Before George, I smell a rat, son Limberham. I doubt, I doubt, here has been some great omission in love affairs.

LIMBERHAM
I think all the stars in heaven have conspired my ruin. I'll look in my almanack.—As I hope for mercy, 'tis cross day now.

Mrs TRICKSY
Hang your pitiful excuses. 'Tis well known what offers I have had, and what fortunes I might have made with others, like a fool as I was, to throw away my youth and beauty upon you. I could have had a young handsome lord, that offered me my coach and six; besides many a good knight and gentleman, that would have parted with their own ladies, and have settled half they had upon me.

LIMBERHAM
Ay, you said so.

Mrs TRICKSY
I said so, sir! Who am I? Is not my word as good as yours?

LIMBERHAM
As mine gentlewoman? though I say it, my word will go for thousands.

Mrs TRICKSY
The more shame for you, that you have done no more for me: But I am resolved I'll not lose my time with you; I'll part.

LIMBERHAM
Do, who cares? Go to Dog-and-Bitch yard, and help your mother to make footmen's shirts.

Mrs TRICKSY
I defy you, slanderer; I defy you.

ALDO
Nay, dear daughter!

LIMBERHAM
I defy her too.

ALDO
Nay, good son!

Mrs TRICKSY
Let me alone: I'll have him cudgelled by my footman.

[Enter **Mrs SAINTLY**.

Mrs SAINTLY
Bless us! what's here to do? My neighbours will think I keep a nest of unclean birds here.

LIMBERHAM
You had best peach now, and make her house be thought a bawdy-house!

Mrs TRICKSY
No, no: While you are in it, you will secure it from that scandal.—Hark hither, Mrs Saintly. [Whispers.]

LIMBERHAM
Do, tell, tell, no matter for that.

Mrs SAINTLY
Who would have imagined you had been such a kind of man, Mr Limberham! O heaven, O heaven!

[Exit.

LIMBERHAM
So, now you have spit your venom, and the storm's over.

ALDO [Crying.]
That I should ever live to see this day!

Mrs TRICKSY
To show I can live honest, in spite of all mankind, I'll go into a nunnery, and that is my resolution.

LIMBERHAM
Do not hinder her, good father Aldo; I am sure she will come back from France, before she gets half way over to Calais.

ALDO
Nay, but son Limberham, this must not be. A word in private;—you will never get such another woman, for love nor money. Do but look upon her; she is a mistress for an emperor.

LIMBERHAM

Let her be a mistress for a pope, like a whore of Babylon, as she is.

ALDO

Would I were worthy to be a young man, for her sake! She should eat pearls, if she would have them.

LIMBERHAM

She can digest them, and gold too. Let me tell you, father Aldo, she has the stomach of an ostrich.

ALDO

Daughter Tricksy, a word with you.

Mrs TRICKSY

I'll hear nothing: I am for a nunnery.

ALDO

I never saw a woman, before you, but first or last she would be brought to reason. Hark you, child, you will scarcely find so kind a keeper. What if he has some impediment one way? Every body is not a Hercules. You shall have my son Woodall, to supply his wants; but, as long as he maintains you, be ruled by him that bears the purse.

[**LIMBERHAM** SINGING.

I my own jailor was; my only foe,
Who did my liberty forego;
I was a prisoner, because I would be so.

ALDO

Why, look you now, son Limberham, is this a song to be sung at such a time, when I am labouring your reconcilement? Come, daughter Tricksy, you must be ruled; I'll be the peace-maker.

Mrs TRICKSY

No, I'm just going.

LIMBERHAM

The devil take me, if I call you back.

Mrs TRICKSY

And his dam take me, if I return, except you do.

ALDO

So, now you will part, for a mere punctilio! Turn to him, daughter: Speak to her, son: Why should you be so refractory both, to bring my gray hairs with sorrow to the grave?

LIMBERHAM

I'll not be forsworn, I swore first;

Mrs TRICKSY

Thou art a forsworn man, however; for thou sworest to love me eternally.

LIMBERHAM
Yes, I was such a fool, to swear so.

ALDO
And will you have that dreadful oath lie gnawing on your conscience?

Mrs TRICKSY
Let him be damned; and so farewell for ever.—

[Going.]

LIMBERHAM
Pug!

Mrs TRICKSY
Did you call, Mr Limberham?

LIMBERHAM
It may be, ay; it may be, no.

Mrs TRICKSY
Well, I am going to the nunnery; but, to shew I am in charity, I'll pray for you.

ALDO
Pray for him! fy, daughter, fy; is that an answer for a Christian?

LIMBERHAM
What did Pug say? will she pray for me? Well, to shew I am in charity, she shall not pray for me. Come back, Pug. But did I ever think thou couldst have been so unkind to have parted with me? [Cries.

ALDO
Look you, daughter, see how nature works in him.

LIMBERHAM
I'll settle two hundred a-year upon thee, because thou said'st thou would'st pray for me.

ALDO
Before George, son Limberham, you will spoil all, if you underbid so. Come, down with your dust, man: What, shew a base mind, when a fair lady's in question!

LIMBERHAM
Well, if I must give three hundred—

Mrs TRICKSY
No, it is no matter; my thoughts are on a better place.

ALDO

Come, there is no better place than little London. You shall not part for a trifle. What, son Limberham! four hundred a year is a square sum, and you shall give it.

LIMBERHAM

It is a round sum indeed; I wish a three-cornered sum would have served her turn.—Why should you be so pervicacious now, Pug? Pray take three hundred. Nay, rather than part, Pug, it shall be so.—

[She frowns.]

ALDO

It shall be so, it shall be so: Come, now buss, and seal the bargain.

Mrs TRICKSY [Kissing him.]

You see what a good natured fool I am, Mr Limberham, to come back into a wicked world, for love of you.—You will see the writings drawn, father?

ALDO

Ay; and pay the lawyer too. Why, this is as it should be! I'll be at the charge of the reconciling supper.— [To her aside.] Daughter, my son Woodall is waiting for you.—Come away, son Limberham to the temple.

LIMBERHAM

With all my heart, while she is in a good humour: It would cost me another hundred, if I should stay till Pug were in wrath again. Adieu, sweet Pug.—

[Exeunt **ALDO**, and **LIMBERHAM**.]

Mrs TRICKSY

That he should be so silly to imagine I would go into a nunnery! it is likely; I have much nun's flesh about me. But here comes my gentleman.

[Enter **WOODALL**, not seeing her.

WOODALL

Now the wife's returned, and the daughter too, and I have seen them both, and am more distracted than before: I would enjoy all, and have not yet determined with which I should begin. It is but a kind of clergy-covetousness in me, to desire so many; if I stand gaping after pluralities, one of them is in danger to be made a sine cure—[Sees her.] O, fortune has determined for me. It is just here, as it is in the world; the mistress will be served before the wife.

Mrs TRICKSY

How now, sir, are you rehearsing your lingua Franca by yourself, that you walk so pensively?

WOODALL

No faith, madam, I was thinking of the fair lady, who, at parting, bespoke so cunningly of me all my essences.

Mrs TRICKSY

But there are other beauties in the house; and I should be impatient of a rival: for I am apt to be partial to myself, and think I deserve to be preferred before them.

WOODALL

Your beauty will allow of no competition; and I am sure my love could make none.

Mrs TRICKSY

Yes, you have seen Mrs Brainsick; she's a beauty.

WOODALL

You mean, I suppose, the peaking creature, the married woman, with a sideling look, as if one cheek carried more bias than the other?

Mrs TRICKSY

Yes, and with a high nose, as visible as a land-mark.

WOODALL

With one cheek blue, the other red; just like the covering of Lambeth Palace.

Mrs TRICKSY

Nay, but her legs, if you could see them—

WOODALL

She was so foolish to wear short petticoats, and show them. They are pillars, gross enough to support a larger building; of the Tuscan order, by my troth.

Mrs TRICKSY

And her little head, upon that long neck, shows like a traitor's skull upon a pole. Then, for her wit—

WOODALL

She can have none: There's not room enough for a thought to play in.

Mrs TRICKSY

I think indeed I may safely trust you with such charms; and you have pleased me with your description of her.

WOODALL

I wish you would give me leave to please you better. But you transact as gravely with me as a Spaniard; and are losing love, as he does Flanders: you consider and demur, when the monarch is up in arms, and at your gates[6].

Mrs TRICKSY

But to yield upon the first summons, ere you have laid a formal siege—To-morrow may prove a luckier day to you.

WOODALL

Believe me, madam, lovers are not to trust to-morrow. Love may die upon our hands, or opportunity be wanting; 'tis best securing the present hour.

Mrs TRICKSY

No, love's like fruit; it must have time to ripen on the tree; if it be green gathered, 'twill but wither afterwards.

WOODALL

Rather 'tis like gun powder; that which fires quickest, is commonly the strongest.—By this burning kiss—

Mrs TRICKSY

You lovers are such froward children, ever crying for the breast; and, when you have once had it, fall fast asleep in the nurse's arms. And with what face should I look upon my keeper after it?

WOODALL

With the same face that all mistresses look upon theirs. Come, come.

Mrs TRICKSY

But my reputation!

WOODALL

Nay, that's no argument, if I should be so base to tell; for women get good fortunes now-a-days, by losing their credit, as a cunning citizen does by breaking.

Mrs TRICKSY

But, I'm so shame-faced! Well, I'll go in, and hide my blushes.

[Exit.

WOODALL

I'll not be long after you; for I think I have hidden my blushes where I shall never find them.

[Re-enter **Mrs TRICKSY**.

Mrs TRICKSY

As I live, Mr Limberham and father Aldo are just returned; I saw them entering. My settlement will miscarry, if you are found here: What shall we do?

WOODALL

Go you into your bed-chamber, and leave me to my fortune.

Mrs TRICKSY

That you should be so dull! their suspicion will be as strong still: for what should make you here?

WOODALL

The curse on't is too, I bid my man tell the family I was gone abroad; so that, if I am seen, you are infallibly discovered.

[Noise.

Mrs TRICKSY
Hark, I hear them! Here's a chest which I borrowed of Mrs Pleasance; get quickly into it, and I will lock you up: there's nothing in't but clothes of Limberham's, and a box of writings.

WOODALL
I shall be smothered.

Mrs TRICKSY
Make haste, for heaven's sake; they'll quickly be gone, and then—

WOODALL
That then will make a man venture any thing.

[He goes in, and she locks the chest.

[Enter **LIMBERHAM** and **ALDO**.

LIMBERHAM
Dost thou not wonder to see me come again so quickly, Pug?

Mrs TRICKSY
No, I am prepared for any foolish freak of yours: I knew you would have a qualm, when you came to settlement.

LIMBERHAM
Your settlement depends most absolutely on that chest.

Mrs TRICKSY
Father Aldo, a word with you, for heaven's sake.

ALDO
No, no, I'll not whisper. Do not stand in your own light, but produce the keys, daughter.

LIMBERHAM
Be not musty, my pretty St Peter, but produce the keys. I must have the writings out, that concern thy settlement.

Mrs TRICKSY
Now I see you are so reasonable, I'll show you I dare trust your honesty; the settlement shall be deferred till another day.

ALDO
No deferring in these cases, daughter.

Mrs TRICKSY
But I have lost the keys.

LIMBERHAM
That's a jest! let me feel in thy pocket, for I must oblige thee.

Mrs TRICKSY
You shall feel no where: I have felt already and am sure they are lost.

ALDO
But feel again, the lawyer stays.

Mrs TRICKSY
Well, to satisfy you, I will feel.—They are not here—nor here neither.

[She pulls out her handkerchief, and the keys drop after it: **LIMBERHAM** takes them up.

LIMBERHAM
Look you now, Pug! who's in the right? Well, thou art born to be a lucky Pug, in spite of thyself.

Mrs TRICKSY [Aside.]
O, I am ruined!—One word, I beseech you, father Aldo.

ALDO
Not a syllable. What the devil's in you, daughter? Open, son, open.

Mrs TRICKSY [Aloud.]
It shall not be opened; I will have my will, though I lose my settlement. Would I were within the chest! I would hold it down, to spite you. I say again, would I were within the chest, I would hold it so fast, you should not open it.—The best on't is, there's good inkle on the top of the inside, if he have the wit to lay hold on't. [Aside.

LIMBERHAM [Going to open it.]
Before George, I think you have the devil in a string, Pug; I cannot open it, for the guts of me. Hictius doctius! what's here to do? I believe, in my conscience, Pug can conjure: Marry, God bless us all good Christians!

ALDO
Push hard, son.

LIMBERHAM
I cannot push; I was never good at pushing. When I push, I think the devil pushes too. Well, I must let it alone, for I am a fumbler. Here, take the keys, Pug.

Mrs TRICKSY [Aside.]
Then all's safe again.

[Enter **JUDITH** and **GERVASE**.

JUDITH

Madam, Mrs Pleasance has sent for the chest you borrowed of her. She has present occasion for it; and has desired us to carry it away.

LIMBERHAM
Well, that's but reason: If she must have it, she must have it.

Mrs TRICKSY
Tell her, it shall be returned some time to-day; at present we must crave her pardon, because we have some writings in it, which must first be taken out, when we can open it.

LIMBERHAM
Nay, that's but reason too: Then she must not have it.

GERVASE
Let me come to't; I'll break it open, and you may take out your writings.

LIMBERHAM
That's true: 'Tis but reasonable it should be broken open.

Mrs TRICKSY
Then I may be bound to make good the loss.

LIMBERHAM
'Tis unreasonable it should be broken open.

ALDO
Before George, Gervase and I will carry it away; and a smith shall be sent for to my daughter Pleasance's chamber, to open it without damage.

LIMBERHAM
Why, who says against it? Let it be carried; I'm all for reason.

Mrs TRICKSY
Hold; I say it shall not stir.

ALDO
What? every one must have their own; Fiat justitia, aut ruat mundus.

LIMBERHAM
Ay, fiat justitia, Pug: She must have her own; for justitia is Latin for justice.

[**ALDO** and **GERVASE** lift at it.

ALDO
I think the devil's in't.

GERVASE
There's somewhat bounces, like him, in't. 'Tis plaguy heavy; but we'll take t'other heave.

Mrs TRICKSY [Taking hold of the chest.]
Then you shall carry me too.
Help, murder, murder!

[A confused gabbling among them.

[Enter **Mrs SAINTLY**.

Mrs SAINTLY
Verily, I think all hell's broke loose among you. What, a schism in my family! Does this become the purity of my house? What will the ungodly say?

LIMBERHAM
No matter for the ungodly; this is all among ourselves: For, look you, the business is this. Mrs Pleasance has sent for this same business here, which she lent to Pug; now Pug has some private businesses within this business, which she would take out first, and the business will not be opened: and this makes all the business.

Mrs SAINTLY
Verily, I am raised up for a judge amongst you; and I say—

Mrs TRICKSY
I'll have no judge: it shall not go.

ALDO
Why son, why daughter, why Mrs Saintly; are you all mad? Hear me, I am sober, I am discreet; let a smith be sent for hither, let him break open the chest; let the things contained be taken out, and the thing containing be restored.

LIMBERHAM
Now hear me too, for I am sober and discreet; father Aldo is an oracle: It shall be so.

Mrs TRICKSY
Well, to show I am reasonable, I am content. Mr Gervase and I will fetch an instrument from the next smith; in the mean time, let the chest remain where it now stands, and let every one depart the chamber.

LIMBERHAM
That no violence be offered to the person of the chest, in Pug's absence.

ALDO
Then this matter is composed.

Mrs TRICKSY [Aside.]
Now I shall have leisure to instruct his man, and set him free, without discovery. Come, Mr Gervase.

[Exeunt all but **Mrs SAINTLY**.

Mrs SAINTLY

There is a certain motion put into my mind, and it is of good. I have keys here, which a precious brother, a devout blacksmith, made me, and which will open any lock of the same bore. Verily, it can be no sin to unlock this chest therewith, and take from thence the spoils of the ungodly. I will satisfy my conscience, by giving part thereof to the hungry and the needy; some to our pastor, that he may prove it lawful; and some I will sanctify to my own use.

[She unlocks the chest, and **WOODALL** starts up.

WOODALL

Let me embrace you, my dear deliverer! Bless us! is it you, Mrs Saintly?

[She shrieks.

Mrs SAINTLY [Shrieking.]

Heaven of his mercy! Stop thief, stop thief!

WOODALL

What will become of me now?

Mrs SAINTLY

According to thy wickedness, shall it be done unto thee. Have I discovered thy backslidings, thou unfaithful man! thy treachery to me shall be rewarded, verily; for I will testify against thee.

WOODALL

Nay, since you are so revengeful, you shall suffer your part of the disgrace; if you testify against me for adultery, I shall testify against you for theft: There's an eighth for your seventh.

[Noise.

Mrs SAINTLY

Verily, they are approaching: Return to my embraces, and it shall be forgiven thee.

WOODALL

Thank you, for your own sake. Hark! they are coming! cry thief again, and help to save all yet.

Mrs SAINTLY

Stop thief, stop thief!

WOODALL

Thank you for your own sake; but I fear 'tis too late.

[Enter **Mrs TRICKSY** and **LIMBERHAM**.

Mrs TRICKSY [Entering.]

The chest open, and Woodall discovered! I am ruined.

LIMBERHAM
Why all this shrieking, Mrs Saintly?

WOODALL [Rushing him down.]
Stop thief, stop thief! cry you mercy, gentleman, if I have hurt you.

LIMBERHAM [Rising.]
'Tis a fine time to cry a man mercy, when you have beaten his wind out of his body.

Mrs SAINTLY
As I watched the chest, behold a vision rushed out of it, on the sudden; and I lifted up my voice, and shrieked.

LIMBERHAM
A vision, landlady! what, have we Gog and Magog in our chamber?

Mrs TRICKSY
A thief, I warrant you, who had gotten into the chest.

WOODALL
Most certainly a thief; for, hearing my landlady cry out, I flew from my chamber to her help, and met him running down stairs, and then he turned back to the balcony, and leapt into the street.

LIMBERHAM
I thought, indeed, that something held down the chest, when I would have opened it:—But my writings are there still, that's one comfort.—Oh seignioro, are you here?

WOODALL
Do you speak to me, sir?

Mrs SAINTLY
This is Mr Woodall, your new fellow-lodger.

LIMBERHAM
Cry you mercy, sir; I durst have sworn you could have spoken lingua Franca—I thought, in my conscience, Pug, this had been thy Italian merchanto.

WOODALL
Sir, I see you mistake me for some other: I should be happy to be better known to you.

LIMBERHAM
Sir, I beg your pardon, with all my hearto. Before George, I was caught again there! But you are so very like a paltry fellow, who came to sell Pug essences this morning, that one would swear those eyes, and that nose and mouth, belonged to that rascal.

WOODALL
You must pardon me, sir, if I do not much relish the close of your compliment.

Mrs TRICKSY
Their eyes are nothing like:—you'll have a quarrel.

LIMBERHAM
Not very like, I confess.

Mrs TRICKSY
Their nose and mouth are quite different.

LIMBERHAM
As Pug says, they are quite different, indeed; but I durst have sworn it had been he; and, therefore, once again, I demand your pardono.

Mrs TRICKSY
Come, let us go down; by this time Gervase has brought the smith, and then Mrs Pleasance may have her chest. Please you, sir, to bear us company.

WOODALL
At your service, madam.

LIMBERHAM
Pray lead the way, sir.

WOODALL
'Tis against my will, sir; but I must leave you in possession.

[Exeunt.

ACT III

SCENE I

Enter **SAINTLY** and **PLEASANCE**.

PLEASANCE
Never fear it, I'll be a spy upon his actions; he shall neither whisper nor gloat on either of them, but I'll ring him such a peal!

Mrs SAINTLY
Above all things, have a care of him yourself; for surely there is witchcraft betwixt his lips: He is a wolf within the sheepfold; and therefore I will be earnest, that you may not fall.

[Exit.

PLEASANCE

Why should my mother be so inquisitive about this lodger? I half suspect old Eve herself has a mind to be nibbling at the pippin. He makes love to one of them, I am confident; it may be to both; for, methinks, I should have done so, if I had been a man; but the damned petticoats have perverted me to honesty, and therefore I have a grudge to him for the privilege of his sex. He shuns me, too, and that vexes me; for, though I would deny him, I scorn he should not think me worth a civil question.

[Re-enter **WOODALL**, with **Mrs TRICKSY**, **Mrs BRAINSICK**, **JUDITH**, and Music.

Mrs BRAINSICK
Come, your works, your works; they shall have the approbation of Mrs Pleasance.

Mrs TRICKSY
No more apologies; give Judith the words, she sings at sight.

JUDITH
I'll try my skill.

A SONG FROM THE ITALIAN.

By a dismal cypress lying,
Damon cried, all pale and dying,—
Kind is death, that ends my pain,
But cruel she I loved in vain.
The mossy fountains
Murmur my trouble,
And hollow mountains
My groans redouble:
Every nymph mourns me,
Thus while I languish;
She only scorns me,
Who caused my anguish.
No love returning me, but all hope denying;
By a dismal cypress lying,
Like a swan, so sung he dying,—
Kind is death, that ends my pain,
But cruel she I loved in vain.

PLEASANCE
By these languishing eyes, and those simagres of yours, we are given to understand, sir, you have a mistress in this company; come, make a free discovery which of them your poetry is to charm, and put the other out of pain.

Mrs TRICKSY
No doubt 'twas meant to Mrs Brainsick.

Mrs BRAINSICK
We wives are despicable creatures; we know it, madam, when a mistress is in presence.

PLEASANCE

Why this ceremony betwixt you? 'Tis a likely proper fellow, and looks as he could people a new isle of Pines[7].

Mrs BRAINSICK

'Twere a work of charity to convert a fair young schismatick, like you, if 'twere but to gain you to a better opinion of the government.

PLEASANCE

If I am not mistaken in you, too, he has works of charity enough upon his hands already; but 'tis a willing soul, I'll warrant him, eager upon the quarry, and as sharp as a governor of Covent-Garden.

WOODALL

Sure this is not the phrase of your family! I thought to have found a sanctified sister; but I suspect now, madam, that if your mother kept a pension in your father's time, there might be some gentleman-lodger in the house; for I humbly conceive you are of the half-strain at least.

PLEASANCE

For all the rudeness of your language, I am resolved to know upon what voyage you are bound; your privateer of love, you Argier's man, that cruize up and down for prize in the Straitsmouth; which of the vessels would you snap now?

Mrs TRICKSY

We are both under safe convoy, madam; a lover and a husband.

PLEASANCE

Nay, for your part, you are notably guarded, I confess; but keepers have their rooks, as well as gamesters; but they only venture under them till they pick up a sum, and then push for themselves.

WOODALL [Aside.]

A plague of her suspicions; they'll ruin me on that side.

PLEASANCE

So; let but little minx go proud, and the dogs in Covent-Garden have her in the wind immediately; all pursue the scent.

Mrs TRICKSY

Not to a boarding-house, I hope?

PLEASANCE

If they were wise, they would rather go to a brothel-house; for there most mistresses have left behind them their maiden-heads, of blessed memory: and those, which would not go off in that market, are carried about by bawds, and sold at doors, like stale flesh in baskets. Then, for your honesty, or justness, as you call it, to your keepers, your kept-mistress is originally a punk; and let the cat be changed into a lady never so formally, she still retains her natural property of mousing.

Mrs BRAINSICK

You are very sharp upon the mistresses; but I hope you'll spare the wives.

PLEASANCE
Yes, as much as your husbands do after the first month of marriage; but you requite their negligence in household-duties, by making them husbands of the first head, ere the year be over.

WOODALL [Aside.]
She has me there, too!

PLEASANCE
And as for you, young gallant—

WOODALL
Hold, I beseech you! a truce for me.

PLEASANCE
In troth, I pity you; for you have undertaken a most difficult task,—to cozen two women, who are no babies in their art: if you bring it about, you perform as much as he that cheated the very lottery.

WOODALL
Ladies, I am sorry this should happen to you for my sake: She is in a raging fit, you see; 'tis best withdrawing, till the spirit of prophecy has left her.

Mrs TRICKSY
I'll take shelter in my chamber,—whither, I hope, he'll have the grace to follow me. [Aside.

Mrs BRAINSICK
And now I think on't, I have some letters to dispatch.

[Exit **Mrs TRICKSY** and **Mrs BRAINSICK**. severally.

PLEASANCE
Now, good John among the maids, how mean you to bestow your time? Away to your study, I advise you; invoke your muses, and make madrigals upon absence.

WOODALL
I would go to China, or Japan, to be rid of that impetuous clack of yours. Farewell, thou legion of tongues in one woman!

PLEASANCE
Will you not stay, sir? it may be I have a little business with you.

WOODALL
Yes, the second part of the same tune! Strike by yourself, sweet larum; you're true bell-metal I warrant you.

[Exit.

PLEASANCE

This spitefulness of mine will be my ruin: To rail them off, was well enough; but to talk him away, too! O tongue, tongue, thou wert given for a curse to all our sex!

[Enter **JUDITH**.

JUDITH
Madam, your mother would speak with you.

PLEASANCE
I will not come; I'm mad, I think; I come immediately. Well, I'll go in, and vent my passion, by railing at them, and him too.

[Exit.

JUDITH
You may enter in safety, sir; the enemy's marched off.

[Re-enter **WOODALL**.

WOODALL
Nothing, but the love I bear thy mistress, could keep me in the house with such a fury. When will the bright nymph appear?

JUDITH
Immediately; I hear her coming.

WOODALL
That I could find her coming, Mrs Judith!

[Enter **Mrs BRAINSICK**.

You have made me languish in expectation, madam. Was it nothing, do you think, to be so near a happiness, with violent desires, and to be delayed?

Mrs BRAINSICK
Is it nothing, do you think, for a woman of honour, to overcome the ties of virtue and reputation; to do that for you, which I thought I should never have ventured for the sake of any man?

WOODALL
But my comfort is, that love has overcome. Your honour is, in other words, but your good repute; and 'tis my part to take care of that: for the fountain of a woman's honour is in the lover, as that of the subject is in the king.

Mrs BRAINSICK
You had concluded well, if you had been my husband: you know where our subjection lies.

WOODALL

But cannot I be yours without a priest? They were cunning people, doubtless, who began that trade; to have a double hank upon us, for two worlds: that no pleasure here, or hereafter, should be had, without a bribe to them.

Mrs BRAINSICK
Well, I'm resolved, I'll read, against the next time I see you; for the truth is, I am not very well prepared with arguments for marriage; meanwhile, farewell.

WOODALL
I stand corrected; you have reason indeed to go, if I can use my time no better: We'll withdraw if you please, and dispute the rest within.

Mrs BRAINSICK
Perhaps, I meant not so.

WOODALL
I understand your meaning at your eyes. You'll watch, Judith?

Mrs BRAINSICK
Nay, if that were all, I expect not my husband till to-morrow. The truth is, he is so oddly humoured, that, if I were ill inclined, it would half justify a woman; he's such a kind of man!

WOODALL
Or, if he be not, well make him such a kind of man.

Mrs BRAINSICK
So fantastical, so musical, his talk all rapture, and half nonsense: like a clock out of order, set him a-going, and he strikes eternally. Besides, he thinks me such a fool, that I could half resolve to revenge myself, in justification of my wit.

WOODALL
Come, come, no half resolutions among lovers; I'll hear no more of him, till I have revenged you fully. Go out and watch, Judith.

[Exit **JUDITH**.

Mrs BRAINSICK
Yet, I could say, in my defence, that my friends married me to him against my will.

WOODALL
Then let us put your friends, too, into the quarrel: it shall go hard, but I'll give you a revenge for them.

[Enter **JUDITH** again, hastily.

How now? what's the matter?

Mrs BRAINSICK

Can'st thou not speak? hast thou seen a ghost?—As I live, she signs horns! that must be for my husband: he's returned.

[JUDITH looks ghastly, and signs horns.

JUDITH
I would have told you so, if I could have spoken for fear.

Mrs BRAINSICK
Hark, a knocking! What shall we do?

[Knocking.

There's no dallying in this case: here you must not be found, that's certain; but Judith hath a chamber within mine; haste quickly thither; I'll secure the rest.

JUDITH
Follow me, sir.

[Exeunt **WOODALL, JUDITH.**

[Knocking again. She opens: Enter **BRAINSICK.**

BRAINSICK
What's the matter, gentlewoman? Am I excluded from my own fortress; and by the way of barricado? Am I to dance attendance at the door, as if I were some base plebeian groom? I'll have you know, that, when my foot assaults, the lightning and the thunder are not so terrible as the strokes: brazen gates shall tremble, and bolts of adamant dismount from off their hinges, to admit me.

Mrs BRAINSICK
Who would have thought, that 'nown dear would have come so soon? I was even lying down on my bed, and dreaming of him. Tum a' me, and buss, poor dear; piddee buss.

BRAINSICK
I nauseate these foolish feats of love.

Mrs BRAINSICK
Nay, but why should he be so fretful now? and knows I dote on him? to leave a poor dear so long without him, and then come home in an angry humour! indeed I'll ky.

BRAINSICK
Pr'ythee, leave thy fulsome fondness; I have surfeited on conjugal embraces.

Mrs BRAINSICK
I thought so: some light huswife has bewitched him from me: I was a little fool, so I was, to leave a dear behind at Barnet, when I knew the women would run mad for him.

BRAINSICK

I have a luscious air forming, like a Pallas, in my brain-pain: and now thou com'st across my fancy, to disturb the rich ideas, with the yellow jaundice of thy jealousy.

[Noise within.

Hark, what noise is that within, about Judith's bed?

Mrs BRAINSICK
I believe, dear, she's making it.—Would the fool would go! [Aside.

BRAINSICK
Hark, again!

Mrs BRAINSICK [Aside]
I have a dismal apprehension in my head, that he's giving my maid a cast of his office, in my stead. O, how it stings me!

[**WOODALL** sneezes.

BRAINSICK
I'll enter, and find the reason of this tumult.

Mrs BRAINSICK [Holding him.]
Not for the world: there may be a thief there; and should I put 'nown dear in danger of his life?—What shall I do? betwixt the jealousy of my love, and fear of this fool, I am distracted: I must not venture them together, whatever comes on it. [Aside.] Why Judith, I say! come forth, damsel.

WOODALL [Within.]
The danger's over; I may come out safely.

JUDITH [Within.]
Are you mad? you shall not.

Mrs BRAINSICK [Aside.]
So, now I'm ruined unavoidably.

BRAINSICK
Whoever thou art, I have pronounced thy doom; the dreadful Brainsick bares his brawny arm in tearing terror; kneeling queens in vain should beg thy being.—Sa, sa, there.

Mrs BRAINSICK [Aside.]
Though I believe he dares not venture in, yet I must not put it to the trial. Why Judith, come out, come out, huswife.

[Enter **JUDITH**, trembling.

What villain have you hid within?

JUDITH
O Lord, madam, what shall I say?

Mrs BRAINSICK
How should I know what you should say? Mr Brainsick has heard a man's voice within; if you know what he makes there, confess the truth; I am almost dead with fear, and he stands shaking.

BRAINSICK
Terror, I! 'tis indignation shakes me. With this sabre I'll slice him as small as atoms; he shall be doomed by the judge, and damned upon the gibbet.

JUDITH [Kneeling.]
My master's so outrageous! sweet madam, do you intercede for me, and I'll tell you all in private. [Whispers. If I say it is a thief, he'll call up help; I know not what of the sudden to invent.

Mrs BRAINSICK
Let me alone.—And is this all? Why would you not confess it before, Judith? when you know I am an indulgent mistress.

[Laughs.

BRAINSICK
What has she confessed?

Mrs BRAINSICK
A venial love-trespass, dear: 'tis a sweetheart of hers; one that is to marry her; and she was unwilling I should know it, so she hid him in her chamber.

[Enter **ALDO**.

ALDO
What's the matter trow? what, in martial posture, son Brainsick?

JUDITH
Pray, father Aldo, do you beg my pardon of my master. I have committed a fault; I have hidden a gentleman in my chamber, who is to marry me without his friends' consent, and therefore came in private to me.

ALDO
That thou should'st think to keep this secret! why, I know it as well as he that made thee.

Mrs BRAINSICK [Aside.]
Heaven be praised, for this knower of all things! Now will he lie three or four rapping volunteers, rather than be thought ignorant in any thing.

BRAINSICK
Do you know his friends, father Aldo?

ALDO

Know them! I think I do. His mother was an arch-deacon's daughter; as honest a woman as ever broke bread: she and I have been cater-cousins in our youth; we have tumbled together between a pair of sheets, i'faith.

BRAINSICK

An honest woman, and yet you two have tumbled together! Those are inconsistent.

ALDO

No matter for that.

Mrs BRAINSICK

He blunders; I must help him. [Aside.] I warrant 'twas before marriage, that you were so great.

ALDO

Before George, and so it was: for she had the prettiest black mole upon her left ancle, it does me good to think on't! His father was squire What-d'ye-call-him, of what-d'ye-call-em shire. What think you, little Judith? do I know him now?

JUDITH

I suppose you may be mistaken: my servant's father is a knight of Hampshire.

ALDO

I meant of Hampshire. But that I should forget he was a knight, when I got him knighted, at the king's coming in! Two fat bucks, I am sure he sent me.

BRAINSICK

And what's his name?

ALDO

Nay, for that, you must excuse me; I must not disclose little Judith's secrets.

Mrs BRAINSICK

All this while the poor gentleman is left in pain: we must let him out in secret; for I believe the young fellow is so bashful, he would not willingly be seen.

JUDITH

The best way will be, for father Aldo to lend me the key of his door, which opens into my chamber; and so I can convey him out.

ALDO [Giving her a key.]

Do so, daughter. Not a word of my familiarity with his mother, to prevent bloodshed betwixt us: but I have her name down in my almanack, I warrant her.

JUDITH

What, kiss and tell, father Aldo? kiss and tell!

[Exit.

Mrs BRAINSICK
I'll go and pass an hour with Mrs Tricksy.

[Exit.

[Enter **LIMBERHAM**.

BRAINSICK
What, the lusty lover Limberham!

[Enter **WOODALL**, at another door.

ALDO
O here's a monsieur, new come over, and a fellow-lodger; I must endear you two to one another.

BRAINSICK
Sir, 'tis my extreme ambition to be better known to you; you come out of the country I adore. And how does the dear Battist[8]? I long for some of his new compositions in the last opera. A propos! I have had the most happy invention this morning, and a tune trouling in my head; I rise immediately in my night-gown and slippers, down I put the notes slap-dash, made words to them like lightning; and I warrant you have them at the circle in the evening.

WOODALL
All were complete, sir, if S. Andre would make steps to them.

BRAINSICK
Nay, thanks to my genius, that care's over: you shall see, you shall see. But first the air. [Sings.] Is it not very fine? Ha, messieurs!

LIMBERHAM
The close of it is the most ravishing I ever heard!

BRAINSICK
I dwell not on your commendations. What say you, sir? [To **WOODALL**] Is it not admirable? Do you enter into it?

WOODALL
Most delicate cadence!

BRAINSICK
Gad, I think so, without vanity. Battist and I have but one soul. But the close, the close! [Sings it thrice over.] I have words too upon the air; but I am naturally so bashful!

WOODALL
Will you oblige me, sir?

BRAINSICK

You might command me, sir; for I sing too en cavalier: but—

LIMBERHAM
But you would be entreated, and say, Nolo, nolo, nolo, three times, like any bishop, when your mouth waters at the diocese.

BRAINSICK
I have no voice; but since this gentleman commands me, let the words commend themselves. [Sings.
My Phillis is charming—

LIMBERHAM
But why, of all names, would you chuse a Phillis? There have been so many Phillises in songs, I thought there had not been another left, for love or money.

BRAINSICK
If a man should listen to a fop! [Sings.
My Phillis—

ALDO
Before George, I am on t'other side: I think, as good no song, as no Phillis.

BRAINSICK
Yet again!—My Phillis—[Sings.

LIMBERHAM
Pray, for my sake, let it be your Chloris.

BRAINSICK [Looking scornfully at him.]
My Phillis—[Sings.

LIMBERHAM
You had as good call her your Succuba.

BRAINSICK
Morbleu! will you not give me leave? I am full of Phillis.
[Sings.] My Phillis—

LIMBERHAM
Nay, I confess, Phillis is a very pretty name.

BRAINSICK
Diable! Now I will not sing, to spite you. By the world, you are not worthy of it. Well, I have a gentleman's fortune; I have courage, and make no inconsiderable figure in the world: yet I would quit my pretensions to all these, rather than not be author of this sonnet, which your rudeness has irrevocably lost.

LIMBERHAM
Some foolish French quelque chose, I warrant you.

BRAINSICK

Quelque chose! O ignorance, in supreme perfection! he means a kek shose[9].

LIMBERHAM

Why a kek shoes let it be then! and a kek shoes for your song.

BRAINSICK

I give to the devil such a judge. Well, were I to be born again, I would as soon be the elephant, as a wit; he's less a monster in this age of malice. I could burn my sonnet, out of rage.

LIMBERHAM

You may use your pleasure with your own.

WOODALL

His friends would not suffer him: Virgil was not permitted to burn his Æneids.

BRAINSICK

Dear sir, I'll not die ungrateful for your approbation. [Aside to **WOODALL**] You see this fellow? he is an ass already; he has a handsome mistress, and you shall make an ox of him ere long.

WOODALL

Say no more, it shall be done.

LIMBERHAM

Hark you, Mr Woodall; this fool Brainsick grows insupportable; he's a public nuisance; but I scorn to set my wit against him: he has a pretty wife: I say no more; but if you do not graff him—

WOODALL

A word to the wise: I shall consider him, for your sake.

LIMBERHAM

Pray do, sir: consider him much.

WOODALL

Much is the word.—This feud makes well for me. [Aside.

BRAINSICK [To **WOODALL**]

I'll give you the opportunity, and rid you of him.—Come away, little Limberham; you, and I, and father Aldo, will take a turn together in the square.

ALDO

We will follow you immediately.

LIMBERHAM

Yes, we will come after you, bully Brainsick: but I hope you will not draw upon us there.

BRAINSICK

If you fear that, Bilbo shall be left behind.

LIMBERHAM
Nay, nay, leave but your madrigal behind: draw not that upon us, and it is no matter for your sword.

[Exit **BRAINSICK**.

[Enter **Mrs TRICKSY**, and **Mrs BRAINSICK**, with a note for each.

WOODALL [Aside.]
Both together! either of them, apart, had been my business: but I shall never play well at this three-hand game.

LIMBERHAM
O Pug, how have you been passing your time?

Mrs TRICKSY
I have been looking over the last present of orange gloves you made me; and methinks I do not like the scent.—O Lord, Mr Woodall, did you bring those you wear from Paris?

WOODALL
Mine are Roman, madam.

Mrs TRICKSY
The scent I love, of all the world. Pray let me see them.

Mrs BRAINSICK
Nay, not both, good Mrs Tricksy; for I love that scent as well as you.

WOODALL [Pulling them off, and giving each one.]
I shall find two dozen more of women's gloves among my trifles, if you please to accept them, ladies.

Mrs TRICKSY
Look to it; we shall expect them.—Now to put in my billet-doux!

Mrs BRAINSICK
So, now, I have the opportunity to thrust in my note.

Mrs TRICKSY
Here, sir, take your glove again; the perfume's too strong for me.

Mrs BRAINSICK
Pray take the other to it; though I should have kept it for a pawn.

[**Mrs BRAINSICK'S** note falls out, **LIMBERHAM** takes it up.

LIMBERHAM
What have we here? [Reads.] for Mr Woodall!

BOTH WOMEN
Hold, hold, Mr Limberham!

[They snatch it.

ALDO
Before George, son Limberham, you shall read it.

WOODALL
By your favour, sir, but he must not.

Mrs TRICKSY
He'll know my hand, and I am ruined!

Mrs BRAINSICK
Oh, my misfortune! Mr Woodall, will you suffer your secrets to be discovered!

WOODALL
It belongs to one of them, that's certain.—Mr Limberham, I must desire you to restore this letter; it is from my mistress.

Mrs TRICKSY
The devil's in him; will he confess?

WOODALL
This paper was sent me from her this morning; and I was so fond of it, that I left it in my glove: If one of the ladies had found it there, I should have been laughed at most unmercifully.

Mrs BRAINSICK
That's well come off!

LIMBERHAM
My heart was at my mouth, for fear it had been Pug's. [Aside.]—There 'tis again—Hold, hold; pray let me see it once more: a mistress, said you?

ALDO
Yes, a mistress, sir. I'll be his voucher, he has a mistress, and a fair one too.

LIMBERHAM
Do you know it, father Aldo.

ALDO
Know it! I know the match is as good as made already: old Woodall and I are all one. You, son, were sent for over on purpose; the articles for her jointure are all concluded, and a friend of mine drew them.

LIMBERHAM
Nay, if father Aldo knows it, I am satisfied.

ALDO

But how came you by this letter, son Woodall? let me examine you.

WOODALL

Came by it! (pox, he has non-plus'd me!) How do you say I came by it, father Aldo?

ALDO

Why, there's it, now. This morning I met your mistress's father, Mr you know who—

WOODALL

Mr who, sir?

ALDO

Nay, you shall excuse me for that; but we are intimate: his name begins with some vowel or consonant, no matter which: Well, her father gave me this very numerical letter, subscribed, for Mr. Woodall.

LIMBERHAM

Before George, and so it is.

ALDO

Carry me this letter, quoth he, to your son Woodall; 'tis from my daughter such a one, and then whispered me her name.

WOODALL

Let me see; I'll read it once again.

LIMBERHAM

What, are you not acquainted with the contents of it?

WOODALL

O, your true lover will read you over a letter from his mistress, a thousand times.

Mrs TRICKSY

Ay, two thousand, if he be in the humour.

WOODALL

Two thousand! then it must be hers.
[Reads to himself.]
"Away to your chamber immediately, and I'll give my fool the slip."—The fool! that may be either the keeper, or the husband; but commonly the keeper is the greater. Humh! without subscription! It must be Tricksy.—Father Aldo, pr'ythee rid me of this coxcomb.

ALDO

Come, son Limberham, we let our friend Brainsick walk too long alone: Shall we follow him? we must make haste; for I expect a whole bevy of whores, a chamber-full of temptation this afternoon: 'tis my day of audience.

LIMBERHAM

Mr Woodall, we leave you here—you remember?

[Exeunt **LIMBERHAM** and **ALDO**.

WOODALL

Let me alone.—Ladies, your servant; I have a little private business with a friend of mine.

Mrs BRAINSICK

Meaning me.—Well, sir, your servant.

Mrs TRICKSY

Your servant, till we meet again.

[Exeunt severally.

SCENE II.—Mr Woodall's Chamber

Mrs BRAINSICK alone.

Mrs BRAINSICK

My note has taken, as I wished: he will be here immediately. If I could but resolve to lose no time, out of modesty; but it is his part to be violent, for both our credits. Never so little force and ruffling, and a poor weak woman is excused.

[Noise.]

Hark, I hear him coming.—Ah me! the steps beat double: He comes not alone. If it should be my husband with him! where shall I hide myself? I see no other place, but under his bed: I must lie as silently as my fear will suffer me. Heaven send me safe again to my own chamber!

[Creeps under the Bed.

[Enter **WOODALL** and **Mrs TRICKSY**.

WOODALL

Well, fortune at the last is favourable, and now you are my prisoner.

Mrs TRICKSY

After a quarter of an hour, I suppose, I shall have my liberty upon easy terms. But pray let us parley a little first.

WOODALL

Let it be upon the bed then. Please you to sit?

Mrs TRICKSY

No matter where; I am never the nearer to your wicked purpose. But you men are commonly great comedians in love-matters; therefore you must swear, in the first place—

WOODALL
Nay, no conditions: The fortress is reduced to extremity; and you must yield upon discretion, or I storm.

Mrs TRICKSY
Never to love any other woman.

WOODALL
I kiss the book upon it.

[Kisses her. **Mrs BRAINSICK** pinches him from underneath the Bed.]

Oh, are you at your love-tricks already? If you pinch me thus, I shall bite your lip.

Mrs TRICKSY
I did not pinch you: But you are apt, I see, to take any occasion of gathering up more close to me.—Next, you shall not so much as look on Mrs Brainsick.

WOODALL
Have you done? these covenants are so tedious!

Mrs TRICKSY
Nay, but swear then.

WOODALL
I do promise, I do swear, I do any thing.

[**Mrs BRAINSICK**. runs a pin into him.]

Oh, the devil! what do you mean to run pins into me? this is perfect caterwauling.

Mrs TRICKSY
You fancy all this; I would not hurt you for the world. Come, you shall see how well I love you.

[Kisses him: **Mrs BRAINSICK** pricks her.]

Oh! I think you have needles growing in your bed.

[Both rise up.

WOODALL
I will see what is the matter in it.

Mrs SAINTLY [Within.]
Mr Woodall, where are you, verily?

WOODALL

Pox verily her! it is my landlady: Here, hide yourself behind the curtains, while I run to the door, to stop her entry.

Mrs TRICKSY

Necessity has no law; I must be patient.

[She gets into the Bed, and draws the clothes over her.

[Enter **Mrs SAINTLY**.

Mrs SAINTLY

In sadness, gentleman, I can hold no longer: I will not keep your wicked counsel, how you were locked up in the chest; for it lies heavy upon my conscience, and out it must, and shall.

WOODALL

You may tell, but who will believe you? where's your witness?

Mrs SAINTLY

Verily, heaven is my witness.

WOODALL

That's your witness too, that you would have allured me to lewdness, have seduced a hopeful young man, as I am; you would have enticed youth: Mark that, beldam.

Mrs SAINTLY

I care not; my single evidence is enough to Mr Limberham; he will believe me, that thou burnest in unlawful lust to his beloved: So thou shalt be an outcast from my family.

WOODALL

Then will I go to the elders of thy church, and lay thee open before them, that thou didst feloniously unlock that chest, with wicked intentions of purloining: So thou shalt be excommunicated from the congregation, thou Jezebel, and delivered over to Satan.

Mrs SAINTLY

Verily, our teacher will not excommunicate me, for taking the spoils of the ungodly, to clothe him; for it is a judged case amongst us, that a married woman may steal from her husband, to relieve a brother. But yet them mayest atone this difference betwixt us; verily, thou mayest.

WOODALL

Now thou art tempting me again. Well, if I had not the gift of continency, what might become of me?

Mrs SAINTLY

The means have been offered thee, and thou hast kicked with the heel. I will go immediately to the tabernacle of Mr Limberham, and discover thee, O thou serpent, in thy crooked paths.

[Going.

WOODALL

Hold, good landlady, not so fast; let me have time to consider on't; I may mollify, for flesh is frail. An hour or two hence we will confer together upon the premises.

Mrs SAINTLY

Oh, on the sudden, I feel myself exceeding sick! Oh! oh!

WOODALL

Get you quickly to your closet, and fall to your mirabilis; this is no place for sick people. Begone, begone!

Mrs SAINTLY

Verily, I can go no farther.

WOODALL

But you shall, verily. I will thrust you down, out of pure pity.

Mrs SAINTLY

Oh, my eyes grow dim! my heart quops, and my back acheth! here I will lay me down, and rest me.

[Throws herself suddenly down upon the Bed; **Mrs TRICKSY** shrieks, and rises; **Mrs BRAINSICK**. rises from under the Bed in a fright.

WOODALL

So! here's a fine business! my whole seraglio up in arms!

Mrs SAINTLY

So, so; if Providence had not sent me hither, what folly had been this day committed!

Mrs TRICKSY

Oh the old woman in the oven! we both overheard your pious documents: Did we not, Mrs Brainsick?

Mrs BRAINSICK

Yes, we did overhear her; and we will both testify against her.

WOODALL

I have nothing to say for her. Nay, I told her her own; you can both bear me witness. If a sober man cannot be quiet in his own chamber for her—

Mrs TRICKSY

For, you know, sir, when Mrs Brainsick and I over-heard her coming, having been before acquainted with her wicked purpose, we both agreed to trap her in it.

Mrs BRAINSICK

And now she would 'scape herself, by accusing us! but let us both conclude to cast an infamy upon her house, and leave it.

Mrs SAINTLY

Sweet Mr Woodall, intercede for me, or I shall be ruined.

WOODALL

Well, for once I'll be good-natured, and try my interest.—
Pray, ladies, for my sake, let this business go no farther.

Mrs TRICKSY and **Mrs BRAINSICK**

You may command us.

WOODALL

For, look you, the offence was properly to my person; and charity has taught me to forgive my enemies. I hope, Mrs Saintly, this will be a warning to you, to amend your life: I speak like a Christian, as one that tenders the welfare of your soul.

Mrs SAINTLY

Verily, I will consider.

WOODALL

Why, that is well said.—[Aside.] Gad, and so must I too; for my people is dissatisfied, and my government in danger: But this is no place for meditation.—Ladies, I wait on you.

[Exeunt.

ACT IV

SCENE I

Enter **ALDO** and **GEOFFERY**.

ALDO

Despatch, Geoffery, despatch: The outlying punks will be upon us, ere I am in a readiness to give audience. Is the office well provided?

GEOFFREY

The stores are very low, sir: Some dolly petticoats, and manteaus we have; and half a dozen pair of laced shoes, bought from court at second hand.

ALDO

Before George, there is not enough to rig out a mournival of whores: They'll think me grown a mere curmudgeon. Mercy on me, how will this glorious trade be carried on, with such a miserable stock!

GEOFFREY

I hear a coach already stopping at the door.

ALDO

Well, somewhat in ornament for the body, somewhat in counsel for the mind; one thing must help out another, in this bad world: Whoring must go on.

[Enter **Mrs OVERDON**, and her Daughter **PRUE**.

Mrs OVERDON
Ask blessing, Prue: He is the best father you ever had.

ALDO
Bless thee, and make thee a substantial, thriving whore. Have your mother in your eye, Prue; it is good to follow good example. How old are you, Prue? Hold up your head, child.

PRUE
Going o'my sixteen, father Aldo.

ALDO
And you have been initiated but these two years: Loss of time, loss of precious time! Mrs Overdon, how much have you made of Prue, since she has been man's meat?

Mrs OVERDON
A very small matter, by my troth; considering the charges I have been at in her education: Poor Prue was born under an unlucky planet; I despair of a coach for her. Her first maiden-head brought me in but little, the weather-beaten old knight, that bought her of me, beat down the price so low. I held her at an hundred guineas, and he bid ten; and higher than thirty would not rise.

ALDO
A pox of his unlucky handsel! He can but fumble, and will not pay neither.

PRUE
Hang him; I could never endure him, father: He is the filthiest old goat; and then he comes every day to our house, and eats out his thirty guineas; and at three months end, he threw me off.

Mrs OVERDON
And since then, the poor child has dwindled, and dwindled away. Her next maiden-head brought me but ten; and from ten she fell to five; and at last to a single guinea: She has no luck to keeping; they all leave her, the more my sorrow.

ALDO
We must get her a husband then in the city; they bite rarely at a stale whore at this end of the town, new furbished up in a tawdry manteau.

Mrs OVERDON
No: Pray let her try her fortune a little longer in the world first: By my troth, I should be loth to be at all this cost, in her French, and her singing, to have her thrown away upon a husband.

ALDO
Before George, there can come no good of your swearing, Mrs Overdon: Say your prayers, Prue, and go duly to church o'Sundays, you'll thrive the better all the week. Come, have a good heart, child; I will keep thee myself: Thou shalt do my little business; and I'll find thee an able young fellow to do thine.

[Enter **Mrs PAD**.

Daughter Pad, you are welcome: What, you have performed the last Christian office to your keeper; I saw you follow him up the heavy hill to Tyburn. Have you had never a business since his death?

Mrs PAD
No indeed, father; never since execution-day. The night before, we lay together most lovingly in Newgate; and the next morning he lift up his eyes, and prepared his soul with a prayer, while one might tell twenty; and then mounted the cart as merrily, as if he had been going for a purse.

ALDO
You are a sorrowful widow, daughter Pad; but I'll take care of you.—Geoffery, see her rigged out immediately for a new voyage: Look in figure 9, in the upper drawer, and give her out the flowered justacorps, with the petticoat belonging to it.

Mrs PAD
Could you not help to prefer me, father?

ALDO
Let me see—let me see:—Before George, I have it, and it comes as pat too! Go me to the very judge that sate upon him; it is an amorous, impotent old magistrate, and keeps admirably. I saw him leer upon you from the bench: He will tell you what is sweeter than strawberries and cream, before you part.

[Enter **Mrs TERMAGANT**.

Mrs TERMAGANT
O father, I think I shall go mad.

ALDO
You are of the violentest temper, daughter Termagant! When had you a business last?

Mrs TERMAGANT
The last I had was with young Caster, that son-of-a-whore gamester: he brought me to taverns, to draw in young cullies, while he bubbled them at play; and, when he had picked up a considerable sum, and should divide, the cheating dog would sink my share, and swear,—Damn him, he won nothing.

ALDO
Unconscionable villain, to cozen you in your own calling!

Mrs TERMAGANT
When he loses upon the square, he comes home zoundsing and blooding; first beats me unmercifully, and then squeezes me to the last penny. He has used me so, that, Gad forgive me, I could almost forswear my trade. The rogue starves me too: He made me keep Lent last year till Whitsuntide, and out-faced me with oaths it was but Easter. And what mads me most, I carry a bastard of the rogue's in my belly; and now he turns me off, and will not own it.

Mrs OVERDON
Lord, how it quops! you are half a year gone, madam.—

[Laying her hand on her belly.

Mrs TERMAGANT
I feel the young rascal kicking already, like his father.—Oh, there is an elbow thrusting out: I think, in my conscience, he is palming and topping in my belly; and practising for a livelihood, before he comes into the world.

ALDO
Geoffery, set her down in the register, that I may provide her a mid-wife, and a dry and wet nurse: When you are up again, as heaven send you a good hour, we will pay him off at law, i'faith. You have him under black and white, I hope?

Mrs TERMAGANT
Yes, I have a note under his hand for two hundred pounds.

ALDO
A note under his hand! that is a chip in porridge; it is just nothing.—Look, Geoffery, to the figure 12, for old half-shirts for childbed linen.

[Enter **Mrs HACKNEY**.

Mrs HACKNEY
O, madam Termagant, are you here? Justice, father Aldo, justice!

ALDO
Why, what is the matter, daughter Hackney?

Mrs HACKNEY
She has violated the law of nations; for yesterday she inveigled my own natural cully from me, a married lord, and made him false to my bed, father.

Mrs TERMAGANT
Come, you are an illiterate whore. He is my lord now; and, though you call him fool, it is well known he is a critic, gentlewoman. You never read a play in all your life; and I gained him by my wit, and so I'll keep him.

Mrs HACKNEY
My comfort is, I have had the best of him; he can take up no more, till his father dies: And so, much good may do you with my cully, and my clap into the bargain.

ALDO
Then there is a father for your child, my lord's son and heir by Mr Caster. But henceforward, to preserve peace betwixt you, I ordain, that you shall ply no more in my daughter Hackney's quarters: You shall have the city, from White-Chapel to Temple-Bar, and she shall have to Covent-Garden downwards: At the play-houses, she shall ply the boxes, because she has the better face; and you shall have the pit, because you can prattle best out of a vizor mask.

Mrs PAD
Then all friends, and confederates. Now let us have father Aldo's delight, and so adjourn the house.

ALDO
Well said, daughter.—Lift up your voices, and sing like nightingales, you tory rory jades. Courage, I say; as long as the merry pence hold out, you shall none of you die in Shoreditch.

[Enter **WOODALL**.

A hey, boys, a hey! here he comes, that will swinge you all! down, you little jades, and worship him; it is the genius of whoring.

WOODALL
And down went chairs and table, and out went every candle. Ho, brave old patriarch in the middle of the church militant! whores of all sorts; forkers and ruin-tailed: Now come I gingling in with my bells, and fly at the whole covey.

ALDO
A hey, a hey, boys! the town's thy own; burn, ravish, and destroy!

WOODALL
We will have a night of it, like Alexander, when he burnt Persepolis: tuez, tuez, tuez! point de quartier.

[He runs in amongst them, and they scuttle about the room.

[Enter **Mrs SAINTLY, PLEASANCE, JUDITH**, with Broom-sticks.

Mrs SAINTLY
What, in the midst of Sodom! O thou lewd young man! My indignation boils over against these harlots; and thus I sweep them from out my family.

PLEASANCE
Down with the Suburbians, down with them.

ALDO
O spare my daughters, Mrs Saintly! Sweet Mrs Pleasance, spare my flesh and blood!

WOODALL
Keep the door open, and help to secure the retreat, father:
There is no pity to be expected.

[The Whores run out, followed by **Mrs SAINTLY, PLEASANCE**, and **JUDITH**.

ALDO
Welladay, welladay! one of my daughters is big with bastard, and she laid at her gascoins most unmercifully! every stripe she had, I felt it: The first fruit of whoredom is irrecoverably lost!

WOODALL

Make haste, and comfort her.

ALDO
I will, I will; and yet I have a vexatious business, which calls me first another way. The rogue, my son, is certainly come over; he has been seen in town four days ago.

WOODALL
It is impossible: I'll not believe it.

ALDO
A friend of mine met his old man, Giles, this very morning, in quest of me; and Giles assured him, his master is lodged in this very street.

WOODALL
In this very street! how knows he that?

ALDO
He dogged him to the corner of it; and then my son turned back, and threatened him. But I'll find out Giles, and then I'll make such an example of my reprobate!

[Exit.

WOODALL
If Giles be discovered, I am undone!—Why, Gervase, where are you, sirrah! Hey, hey!

[Enter **GERVASE**.

Run quickly to that betraying rascal Giles, a rogue, who would take Judas's bargain out of his hands, and undersell him. Command him strictly to mew himself up in his lodgings, till farther orders: and in case he be refractory, let him know, I have not forgot to kick and cudgel. That memento would do well for you too, sirrah.

GERVASE
Thank your worship; you have always been liberal of your hands to me.

WOODALL
And you have richly deserved it.

GERVASE
I will not say, who has better deserved it of my old master.

WOODALL
Away, old Epictetus, about your business, and leave your musty morals, or I shall—

GERVASE
Nay, I won't forfeit my own wisdom so far as to suffer for it.
Rest you merry: I'll do my best, and heaven mend all.

[Exit.

[Enter **Mrs SAINTLY**.

Mrs SAINTLY
Verily, I have waited till you were alone, and am come to rebuke you, out of the zeal of my spirit.

WOODALL
It is the spirit of persecution. Dioclesian, and Julian the apostate, were but types of thee. Get thee hence, thou old Geneva testament: thou art a part of the ceremonial law, and hast been abolished these twenty years.

Mrs SAINTLY
All this is nothing, sir. I am privy to your plots: I'll discover them to Mr Limberham, and make the house too hot for you.

WOODALL
What, you can talk in the language of the world, I see!

Mrs SAINTLY
I can, I can, sir; and in the language of the flesh and devil too, if you provoke me to despair: You must, and shall be mine, this night.

WOODALL
The very ghost of queen Dido in the ballad.[10]

Mrs SAINTLY
Delay no longer, or—

WOODALL
Or! you will not swear, I hope?

Mrs SAINTLY
Uds-niggers but I will; and that so loud, that Mr Limberham shall hear me.

WOODALL
Uds-niggers, I confess, is a very dreadful oath. You could lie naturally before, as you are a fanatic; if you can swear such rappers too, there is hope of you; you may be a woman of the world in time. Well, you shall be satisfied, to the utmost farthing, to-night, and in your own chamber.

Mrs SAINTLY
Or, expect to-morrow—

WOODALL
All shall be atoned ere then. Go, provide the bottle of clary, the Westphalia ham, and other fortifications of nature; we shall see what may be done. What! an old woman must not be cast away.

[Chucks her.

Mrs SAINTLY
Then, verily, I am appeased.

WOODALL
Nay, no relapsing into verily; that is in our bargain. Look how she weeps for joy! It is a good old soul, I warrant her.

Mrs SAINTLY
You will not fail?

WOODALL
Dost thou think I have no compassion for thy gray hairs? Away, away; our love may be discovered: We must avoid scandal; it is thy own maxim.

[Exit **Mrs SAINTLY**.

They are all now at ombre; and Brainsick's maid has promised to send her mistress up.

[Enter **PLEASANCE**.

That fury here again!

PLEASANCE [Aside.]
I'll conquer my proud spirit, I am resolved on it, and speak kindly to him.—What, alone, sir! If my company be not troublesome; or a tender young creature, as I am, may safely trust herself with a man of such prowess, in love affairs—It wonnot be.

WOODALL [Aside.
So! there is one broadside already: I must sheer off.

PLEASANCE
What, you have been pricking up and down here upon a cold scent[11]; but, at last, you have hit it off, it seems! Now for a fair view at the wife or mistress: up the wind, and away with it: Hey, Jowler!—I think I am bewitched, I cannot hold.

WOODALL
Your servant, your servant, madam: I am in a little haste at present.

[Going.

PLEASANCE
Pray resolve me first, for which of them you lie in ambush; for, methinks, you have the mien of a spider in her den. Come, I know the web is spread, and whoever comes, Sir Cranion stands ready to dart out, hale her in, and shed his venom.

WOODALL [Aside.]
But such a terrible wasp, as she, will spoil the snare, if I durst tell her so.

PLEASANCE

It is unconscionably done of me, to debar you the freedom and civilities of the house. Alas, poor gentleman! to take a lodging at so dear a rate, and not to have the benefit of his bargain!—Mischief on me, what needed I have said that? [Aside.

WOODALL

The dialogue will go no farther. Farewell, gentle, quiet lady.

PLEASANCE

Pray stay a little; I'll not leave you thus.

WOODALL

I know it; and therefore mean to leave you first.

PLEASANCE

O, I find it now! you are going to set up your bills, like a love-mountebank, for the speedy cure of distressed widows, old ladies, and languishing maids in the green-sickness: a sovereign remedy.

WOODALL

That last, for maids, would be thrown away: Few of your age are qualified for the medicine. What the devil would you be at, madam?

PLEASANCE

I am in the humour of giving you good counsel. The wife can afford you but the leavings of a fop; and to a witty man, as you think yourself, that is nauseous: The mistress has fed upon a fool so long, she is carrion too, and common into the bargain. Would you beat a ground for game in the afternoon, when my lord mayor's pack had been before you in the morning?

WOODALL

I had rather sit five hours at one of his greasy feasts, then hear you talk.

PLEASANCE

Your two mistresses keep both shop and warehouse; and what they cannot put off in gross, to the keeper and the husband, they sell by retail to the next chance-customer. Come, are you edified?

WOODALL

I am considering how to thank you for your homily; and, to make a sober application of it, you may have some laudable design yourself in this advice.

PLEASANCE

Meaning, some secret inclination to that amiable person of yours?

WOODALL

I confess, I am vain enough to hope it; for why should you remove the two dishes, but to make me fall more hungrily on the third?

PLEASANCE

Perhaps, indeed, in the way of honour—

WOODALL
Paw, paw! that word honour has almost turned my stomach: it carries a villainous interpretation of matrimony along with it. But, in a civil way, I could be content to deal with you, as the church does with the heads of your fanatics, offer you a lusty benefice to stop your mouth; if fifty guineas, and a courtesy more worth, will win you.

PLEASANCE
Out upon thee! fifty guineas! Dost thou think I'll sell myself? And at a playhouse price too? Whenever I go, I go all together: No cutting from the whole piece; he who has me shall have the fag-end with the rest, I warrant him. Be satisfied, thy sheers shall never enter into my cloth. But, look to thyself, thou impudent belswagger: I will be revenged; I will.

[Exit.

WOODALL
The maid will give warning, that is my comfort; for she is bribed on my side. I have another kind of love to this girl, than to either of the other two; but a fanatic's daughter, and the noose of matrimony, are such intolerable terms! O, here she comes, who will sell me better cheap.

SCENE Opens to Brainsick's Apartment

Enter **Mrs BRAINSICK**.

Mrs BRAINSICK
How now, sir? what impudence is this of yours, to approach my lodgings?

WOODALL
You lately honoured mine; and it is the part of a well-bred man, to return your visit.

Mrs BRAINSICK
If I could have imagined how base a fellow you had been, you should not then have been troubled with my company.

WOODALL
How could I guess, that you intended me the favour, without first acquainting me?

Mrs BRAINSICK
Could I do it, ungrateful as you are, with more obligation to you, or more hazard to myself, than by putting my note into your glove?

WOODALL
Was it yours, then? I believed it came from Mrs Tricksy.

Mrs BRAINSICK

You wished it so; which made you so easily believe it. I heard the pleasant dialogue betwixt you.

WOODALL

I am glad you did; for you could not but observe, with how much care I avoided all occasions of railing at you; to which she urged me, like a malicious woman, as she was.

Mrs BRAINSICK

By the same token, you vowed and swore never to look on Mrs Brainsick!

WOODALL

But I had my mental reservations in a readiness. I had vowed fidelity to you before; and there went my second oath, i'faith: it vanished in a twinkling, and never gnawed my conscience in the least.

Mrs BRAINSICK

Well, I shall never heartily forgive you.

JUDITH [Within.]

Mr Brainsick, Mr Brainsick, what do you mean, to make my lady lose her game thus? Pray, come back, and take up her cards again.

Mrs BRAINSICK

My husband, as I live! Well, for all my quarrel to you, step immediately into that little dark closet: it is for my private occasions; there is no lock, but he will not stay.

WOODALL

Thus am I ever tantalized!

[Goes in.

[Enter **BRAINSICK**.

BRAINSICK

What, am I become your drudge? your slave? the property of all your pleasures? Shall I, the lord and master of your life, become subservient; and the noble name of husband be dishonoured? No, though all the cards were kings and queens, and Indies to be gained by every deal—

Mrs BRAINSICK

My dear, I am coming to do my duty. I did but go up a little, (I whispered you for what) and am returning immediately.

BRAINSICK

Your sex is but one universal ordure, a nuisance, and incumbrance of that majestic creature, man: yet I myself am mortal too. Nature's necessities have called me up; produce your utensil of urine.

Mrs BRAINSICK

It is not in the way, child: You may go down into the garden.

BRAINSICK

The voyage is too far: though the way were paved with pearls and diamonds, every step of mine is precious, as the march of monarchs.

Mrs BRAINSICK
Then my steps, which are not so precious, shall be employed for you: I will call up Judith.

BRAINSICK
I will not dance attendance. At the present, your closet shall be honoured.

Mrs BRAINSICK
O lord, dear, it is not worthy to receive such a man as you are.

BRAINSICK
Nature presses; I am in haste.

Mrs BRAINSICK
He must be discovered, and I unavoidably undone! [Aside.

[**BRAINSICK** goes to the door, and **WOODALL** meets him: She shrieks out.

BRAINSICK
Monsieur Woodall!

WOODALL
Sir, begone, and make no noise, or you will spoil all.

BRAINSICK
Spoil all, quotha! what does he mean, in the name of wonder?

WOODALL [Taking him aside.]
Hark you, Mr Brainsick, is the devil in you, that you and your wife come hither, to disturb my intrigue, which you yourself engaged me in, with Mrs Tricksy, to revenge you on Limberham? Why, I had made an appointment with her here; but, hearing somebody come up, I retired into the closet, till I was satisfied it was not the keeper.

BRAINSICK
But why this intrigue in my wife's chamber?

WOODALL
Why, you turn my brains, with talking to me of your wife's chamber! do you lie in common? the wife and husband, the keeper and the mistress?

Mrs BRAINSICK
I am afraid they are quarrelling; pray heaven I get off.

BRAINSICK
Once again, I am the sultan of this place: Mr Limberham is the mogul of the next mansion.

WOODALL

Though I am a stranger in the house, it is impossible I should be so much mistaken: I say, this is Limberham's lodging.

BRAINSICK

You would not venture a wager of ten pounds, that you are not mistaken?

WOODALL

It is done: I will lay you.

BRAINSICK

Who shall be judge?

WOODALL

Who better than your wife? She cannot be partial, because she knows not on which side you have laid.

BRAINSICK

Content.—Come hither, lady mine: Whose lodgings are these? who is lord, and grand seignior of them?

Mrs BRAINSICK [Aside.]

Oh, goes it there?—Why should you ask me such a question, when every body in the house can tell they are 'nown dear's?

BRAINSICK

Now are you satisfied? Children and fools, you know the proverb—

WOODALL

Pox on me! nothing but such a positive coxcomb as I am, would have laid his money upon such odds; as if you did not know your own lodgings better than I, at half a day's warning! And that which vexes me more than the loss of my money, is the loss of my adventure!

[Exit.

BRAINSICK

It shall be spent: We will have a treat with it. This is a fool of the first magnitude.

Mrs BRAINSICK

Let my own dear alone, to find a fool out.

[Enter **LIMBERHAM**.

LIMBERHAM

Bully Brainsick, Pug has sent me to you on an embassy, to bring you down to cards again; she is in her mulligrubs already; she will never forgive you the last vol you won. It is but losing a little to her, out of complaisance, as they say, to a fair lady; and whatever she wins, I will make up to you again in private.

BRAINSICK

I would not be that slave you are, to enjoy the treasures of the east. The possession of Peru, and of Potosi, should not buy me to the bargain.

LIMBERHAM
Will you leave your perboles, and come then?

BRAINSICK
No; for I have won a wager, to be spent luxuriously at Long's; with Pleasance of the party, and Termagant Tricksy; and I will pass, in person, to the preparation: Come, matrimony.

[Exeunt **BRAINSICK**, Mrs **BRAINSICK**.

[Enter **Mrs SAINTLY**, and **PLEASANCE**.

PLEASANCE
To him: I'll second you: now for mischief!

Mrs SAINTLY
Arise, Mr Limberham, arise; for conspiracies are hatched against you, and a new Faux is preparing to blow up your happiness.

LIMBERHAM
What is the matter, landlady? Pr'ythee, speak good honest English, and leave thy canting.

Mrs SAINTLY
Verily, thy beloved is led astray, by the young man Woodall, that vessel of uncleanness: I beheld them communing together; she feigned herself sick, and retired to her tent in the garden-house; and I watched her out-going, and behold he followed her.

PLEASANCE
Do you stand unmoved, and hear all this?

LIMBERHAM
Before George, I am thunder-struck!

Mrs SAINTLY
Take to thee thy resolution, and avenge thyself.

LIMBERHAM
But give me leave to consider first: A man must do nothing rashly.

PLEASANCE
I could tear out the villain's eyes, for dishonouring you, while you stand considering, as you call it. Are you a man, and suffer this?

LIMBERHAM
Yes, I am a man; but a man's but a man, you know: I am recollecting myself, how these things can be.

Mrs SAINTLY

How they can be! I have heard them; I have seen them.

LIMBERHAM

Heard them, and seen them! It may be so; but yet I cannot enter into this same business: I am amazed, I must confess; but the best is, I do not believe one word of it.

Mrs SAINTLY

Make haste, and thine own eyes shall testify against her.

LIMBERHAM

Nay, if my own eyes testify, it may be so:—but it is impossible, however; for I am making a settlement upon her, this very day.

PLEASANCE

Look, and satisfy yourself, ere you make that settlement on so false a creature.

LIMBERHAM

But yet, if I should look, and not find her false, then I must cast in another hundred, to make her satisfaction.

PLEASANCE

Was there ever such a meek, hen-hearted creature!

Mrs SAINTLY

Verily, thou has not the spirit of a cock-chicken.

LIMBERHAM

Before George, but I have the spirit of a lion, and I will tear her limb from limb—if I could believe it.

PLEASANCE

Love, jealousy, and disdain, how they torture me at once! And this insensible creature—were I but in his place—[To him.] Think, that this very instant she is yours no more: Now, now she is giving up herself, with so much violence of love, that if thunder roared, she could not hear it.

LIMBERHAM

I have been whetting all this while: They shall be so taken in the manner, that Mars and Venus shall be nothing to them.

PLEASANCE

Make haste; go on then.

LIMBERHAM

Yes, I will go on;—and yet my mind misgives me plaguily.

Mrs SAINTLY

Again backsliding!

PLEASANCE
Have you no sense of honour in you?

LIMBERHAM
Well, honour is honour, and I must go: But I shall never get me such another Pug again! O, my heart! my poor tender heart! it is just breaking with Pug's unkindness!

[They drag him out.

SCENE II.—Woodall and Mrs Tricksy Discovered in the Garden-House

Enter **GERVASE** to them.

GERVASE
Make haste, and save yourself, sir; the enemy's at hand: I have discovered him from the corner, where you set me sentry.

WOODALL
Who is it?

GERVASE
Who should it be, but Limberham? armed with a two-hand fox. O Lord, O Lord!

Mrs TRICKSY
Enter quickly into the still-house, both of you, and leave me to him: There is a spring-lock within, to open it when we are gone.

WOODALL
Well, I have won the party and revenge, however: A minute longer, and I had won the tout.

[They go in: She locks the Door.

[Enter **LIMBERHAM**, with a great Sword.

LIMBERHAM
Disloyal Pug!

Mrs TRICKSY
What humour is this? you are drunk, it seems: Go sleep.

LIMBERHAM
Thou hast robbed me of my repose for ever: I am like Macbeth, after the death of good king Duncan; methinks a voice says to me,—Sleep no more; Tricksy has murdered sleep.

Mrs TRICKSY

Now I find it: You are willing to save your settlement, and are sent by some of your wise counsellors, to pick a quarrel with me.

LIMBERHAM

I have been your cully above these seven years; but, at last, my eyes are opened to your witchcraft; and indulgent heaven has taken care of my preservation. In short, madam, I have found you out; and, to cut off preambles, produce your adulterer.

Mrs TRICKSY

If I have any, you know him best: You are the only ruin of my reputation. But if I have dishonoured my family, for the love of you, methinks you should be the last man to upbraid me with it.

LIMBERHAM

I am sure you are of the family of your abominable great grandam Eve; but produce the man, or, by my father's soul—

Mrs TRICKSY

Still I am in the dark.

LIMBERHAM

Yes, you have been in the dark; I know it: But I shall bring you to light immediately.

Mrs TRICKSY

You are not jealous?

LIMBERHAM

No; I am too certain to be jealous: But you have a man here, that shall be nameless; let me see him.

Mrs TRICKSY

Oh, if that be your business, you had best search: And when you have wearied yourself, and spent your idle humour, you may find me above, in my chamber, and come to ask my pardon.

[Going.

LIMBERHAM

You may go, madam; but I shall beseech your ladyship to leave the key of the still-house door behind you: I have a mind to some of the sweet-meats you have locked up there; you understand me. Now, for the old dog-trick! you have lost the key, I know already, but I am prepared for that; you shall know you have no fool to deal with.

Mrs TRICKSY

No; here is the key: Take it, and satisfy your foolish curiosity.

LIMBERHAM [Aside.]

This confidence amazes me! If those two gipsies have abused me, and I should not find him there now, this would make an immortal quarrel.

Mrs TRICKSY [Aside.]

I have put him to a stand.

LIMBERHAM
Hang it, it is no matter; I will be satisfied: If it comes to a rupture, I know the way to buy my peace. Pug, produce the key.

Mrs TRICKSY [Takes him about the neck.]
My dear, I have it for you: come, and kiss me. Why would you be so unkind to suspect my faith now! when I have forsaken all the world for you.—

[Kiss again.]

But I am not in the mood of quarrelling to-night; I take this jealousy the best way, as the effect of your passion. Come up, and we will go to bed together, and be friends.

[Kiss again.

LIMBERHAM [Aside.]
Pug is in a pure humour to-night, and it would vex a man to lose it; but yet I must be satisfied:—and therefore, upon mature consideration, give me the key.

Mrs TRICKSY
You are resolved, then?

LIMBERHAM
Yes, I am resolved; for I have sworn to myself by Styx; and that is an irrevocable oath.

Mrs TRICKSY
Now, see your folly: There's the key.

[Gives it him.

LIMBERHAM
Why, that is a loving Pug; I will prove thee innocent immediately: And that will put an end to all controversies betwixt us.

Mrs TRICKSY
Yes, it shall put an end to all our quarrels: Farewell for the last time, sir. Look well upon my face, that you may remember it; for, from this time forward, I have sworn it irrevocably too, that you shall never see it more.

LIMBERHAM
Nay, but hold a little, Pug. What's the meaning of this new commotion?

Mrs TRICKSY
No more; but satisfy your foolish fancy, for you are master: and, besides, I am willing to be justified.

LIMBERHAM

Then you shall be justified.

[Puts the Key in the Door.

Mrs TRICKSY
I know I shall: Farewell.

LIMBERHAM
But, are you sure you shall?

Mrs TRICKSY
No, no, he is there: You'll find him up in the chimney, or behind the door; or, it may be, crowded into some little galley-pot.

LIMBERHAM
But you will not leave me, if I should look?

Mrs TRICKSY
You are not worthy my answer: I am gone.

[Going out.

LIMBERHAM
Hold, hold, divine Pug, and let me recollect a little.—This is no time for meditation neither: while I deliberate, she may be gone. She must be innocent, or she could never be so confident and careless.— Sweet Pug, forgive me.

[Kneels.

Mrs TRICKSY
I am provoked too far.

LIMBERHAM
It is the property of a goddess to forgive. Accept of this oblation; with this humble kiss, I here present it to thy fair hand: I conclude thee innocent without looking, and depend wholly upon thy mercy.

[Offers the Key.

Mrs TRICKSY
No, keep it, keep it: the lodgings are your own.

LIMBERHAM
If I should keep it, I were unworthy of forgiveness: I will no longer hold this fatal instrument of our separation.

Mrs TRICKSY [Taking it.]
Rise, sir: I will endeavour to overcome my nature, and forgive you; for I am so scrupulously nice in love, that it grates my very soul to be suspected: Yet, take my counsel, and satisfy yourself.

LIMBERHAM
I would not be satisfied, to be possessor of Potosi, as my brother Brainsick says. Come to bed, dear Pug.—Now would not I change my condition, to be an eastern monarch!

[Exeunt.

[Enter **WOODALL** and **GERVASE**.

GERVASE
O lord, sir, are we alive!

WOODALL
Alive! why, we were never in any danger: Well, she is a rare manager of a fool!

GERVASE
Are you disposed yet to receive good counsel? Has affliction wrought upon you?

WOODALL
Yes, I must ask thy advice in a most important business. I have promised a charity to Mrs Saintly, and she expects it with a beating heart a-bed: Now, I have at present no running cash to throw away; my ready money is all paid to Mrs Tricksy, and the bill is drawn upon me for to-night.

GERVASE
Take advice of your pillow.

WOODALL
No, sirrah; since you have not the grace to offer yours, I will for once make use of my authority and command you to perform the foresaid drudgery in my place.

GERVASE
Zookers, I cannot answer it to my conscience.

WOODALL
Nay, an your conscience can suffer you to swear, it shall suffer you to lie too: I mean in this sense. Come, no denial, you must do it; she is rich, and there is a provision for your life.

GERVASE
I beseech you, sir, have pity on my soul.

WOODALL
Have you pity of your body: There is all the wages you must expect.

GERVASE
Well, sir, you have persuaded me: I will arm my conscience with a resolution of making her an honourable amends by marriage; for to-morrow morning a parson shall authorise my labours, and turn fornication into duty. And, moreover, I will enjoin myself, by way of penance, not to touch her for seven nights after.

WOODALL

Thou wert predestinated for a husband, I see, by that natural instinct: As we walk, I will instruct thee how to behave thyself, with secrecy and silence.

GERVASE

I have a key of the garden, to let us out the back-way into the street, and so privately to our lodging.

WOODALL

'Tis well: I will plot the rest of my affairs a-bed; for it is resolved that Limberham shall not wear horns alone: and I am impatient till I add to my trophy the spoils of Brainsick.

[Exeunt.

ACT V

SCENE I

Enter **WOODALL** and **JUDITH**.

JUDITH

Well, you are a lucky man! Mrs Brainsick is fool enough to believe you wholly innocent; and that the adventure of the garden-house, last night, was only a vision of Mrs Saintly's.

WOODALL

I knew, if I could once speak with her, all would be set right immediately; for, had I been there, look you—

JUDITH

As you were, most certainly.

WOODALL

Limberham must have found me out; that fe-fa-fum of a keeper would have smelt the blood of a cuckold-maker: They say, he was peeping and butting about in every cranny.

JUDITH

But one. You must excuse my unbelief, though Mrs Brainsick is better satisfied. She and her husband, you know, went out this morning to the New Exchange: There she has given him the slip; and pretending to call at her tailor's to try her stays for a new gown—

WOODALL

I understand thee;—she fetched me a short turn, like a hare before her muse, and will immediately run hither to covert?

JUDITH

Yes; but because your chamber will be least suspicious, she appoints to meet you there; that, if her husband should come back, he may think her still abroad, and you may have time—

WOODALL
To take in the horn-work. It happens as I wish; for Mrs Tricksy, and her keeper, are gone out with father Aldo, to complete her settlement; my landlady is safe at her morning exercise with my man Gervase, and her daughter not stirring: the house is our own, and iniquity may walk bare-faced.

JUDITH
And, to make all sure, I am ordered to be from home. When I come back again, I shall knock at your door, with, Speak, brother, speak;
[Singing.
Is the deed done?

WOODALL
Long ago, long ago;—and then we come panting out together.
Oh, I am ravished with the imagination on't!

JUDITH
Well, I must retire; good-morrow to you, sir.

[Exit.

WOODALL
Now do I humbly conceive, that this mistress in matrimony will give me more pleasure than the former; for your coupled spaniels, when they are once let loose, are afterwards the highest rangers.

[Enter **Mrs BRAINSICK**, running.

Mrs BRAINSICK
Oh dear Mr Woodall, what shall I do?

WOODALL
Recover breath, and I'll instruct you in the next chamber.

Mrs BRAINSICK
But my husband follows me at heels.

WOODALL
Has he seen you?

Mrs BRAINSICK
I hope not: I thought I had left him sure enough at the Exchange; but, looking behind me, as I entered into the house, I saw him walking a round rate this way.

WOODALL
Since he has not seen you, there is no danger; you need but step into my chamber, and there we will lock ourselves up, and transform him in a twinkling.

Mrs BRAINSICK
I had rather have got into my own; but Judith is gone out with the key, I doubt.

WOODALL
Yes, by your appointment. But so much the better; for when the cuckold finds no company, he will certainly go a sauntering again.

Mrs BRAINSICK
Make haste, then.

WOODALL
Immediately.—

[Goes to open the Door hastily, and breaks his Key.]

What is the matter here? the key turns round, and will not open! As I live, we are undone! with too much haste it is broken!

Mrs BRAINSICK
Then I am lost; for I cannot enter into my own.

WOODALL
This next room is Limberham's. See! the door's open; and he and his mistress are both abroad.

Mrs BRAINSICK
There is no remedy, I must venture in; for his knowing I am come back so soon, must be cause of jealousy enough, if the fool should find me.

WOODALL [Looking in.]
See there! Mrs Tricksy has left her Indian gown upon the bed; clap it on, and turn your back: he will easily mistake you for her, if he should look in upon you.

Mrs BRAINSICK
I will put on my vizor-mask, however, for more security.

[Noise.]

Hark! I hear him.

[Goes in.

[Enter **BRAINSICK**.

BRAINSICK
What, in a musty musing, monsieur Woodall! Let me enter into the affair.

WOODALL

You may guess it, by the post I have taken up.

BRAINSICK

O, at the door of the damsel Tricksy! your business is known by your abode; as the posture of a porter before a gate, denotes to what family he belongs. [Looks in.] It is an assignation, I see; for yonder she stands, with her back toward me, drest up for the duel, with all the ornaments of the east. Now for the judges of the field, to divide the sun and wind betwixt the combatants, and a tearing trumpeter to sound the charge.

WOODALL

It is a private quarrel, to be decided without seconds; and therefore you would do me a favour to withdraw.

BRAINSICK

Your Limberham is nearer than you imagine: I left him almost entering at the door.

WOODALL

Plague of all impertinent cuckolds! they are ever troublesome to us honest lovers: so intruding!

BRAINSICK

They are indeed, where their company is not desired.

WOODALL

Sure he has some tutelar devil to guard his brows! just when she had bobbed him, and made an errand home, to come to me!

BRAINSICK

It is unconscionably done of him. But you shall not adjourn your love for this: the Brainsick has an ascendant over him; I am your guarantee; he is doomed a cuckold, in disdain of destiny.

WOODALL

What mean you?

BRAINSICK

To stand before the door with my brandished blade, and defend the entrance: He dies upon the point, if he approaches.

WOODALL

If I durst trust it, it is heroic.

BRAINSICK

It is the office of a friend: I will do it.

WOODALL [Aside.]

Should he know hereafter his wife were here, he would think I had enjoyed her, though I had not; it is best venturing for something. He takes pains enough, on conscience, for his cuckoldom; and, by my troth, has earned it fairly.—But, may a man venture upon your promise?

BRAINSICK

Bars of brass, and doors of adamant, could not more secure you.

WOODALL

I know it; but still gentle means are best: You may come to force at last. Perhaps you may wheedle him away: it is but drawing a trope or two upon him.

BRAINSICK

He shall have it, with all the artillery of eloquence.

WOODALL

Ay, ay; your figure breaks no bones. With your good leave.—

[Goes in.

BRAINSICK

Thou hast it, boy. Turn to him, madam; to her Woodall: and St George for merry England. Tan ta ra ra ra, ra ra! Dub, a dub, dub; Tan ta ra ra ra.

[Enter **LIMBERHAM**.

LIMBERHAM

How now, bully Brainsick! What, upon the Tan ta ra, by yourself?

BRAINSICK

Clangor, taratantara, murmur.

LIMBERHAM

Commend me to honest lingua Franca. Why, this is enough to stun a Christian, with your Hebrew, and your Greek, and such like Latin.

BRAINSICK

Out, ignorance!

LIMBERHAM

Then ignorance, by your leave; for I must enter.

[Attempts to pass.

BRAINSICK

Why in such haste? the fortune of Greece depends not on it.

LIMBERHAM

But Pug's fortune does: that is dearer to me than Greece, and sweeter than ambergrease.

BRAINSICK

You will not find her here. Come, you are jealous; you are haunted with a raging fiend, that robs you of your sweet repose.

LIMBERHAM
Nay, an you are in your perbole's again! Look you, it is Pug is jealous of her jewels: she has left the key of her cabinet behind, and has desired me to bring it back to her.

BRAINSICK
Poor fool! he little thinks she is here before him!—Well, this pretence will never pass on me; for I dive deeper into your affairs; you are jealous. But, rather than my soul should be concerned for a sex so insignificant—Ha! the gods! If I thought my proper wife were now within, and prostituting all her treasures to the lawless love of an adulterer, I would stand as intrepid, as firm, and as unmoved, as the statue of a Roman gladiator.

LIMBERHAM [In the same tone.]
Of a Roman gladiator!—Now are you as mad as a March hare; but I am in haste, to return to Pug: yet, by your favour, I will first secure the cabinet.

BRAINSICK
No, you must not.

LIMBERHAM
Must not? What, may not a man come by you, to look upon his own goods and chattels, in his own chamber?

BRAINSICK
No; with this sabre I defy the destinies, and dam up the passage with my person; like a rugged rock, opposed against the roaring of the boisterous billows. Your jealousy shall have no course through me, though potentates and princes—

LIMBERHAM
Pr'ythee, what have we to do with potentates and princes? Will you leave your troping, and let me pass?

BRAINSICK
You have your utmost answer.

LIMBERHAM
If this maggot bite a little deeper, we shall have you a citizen of Bethlem yet, ere dog-days. Well, I say little; but I will tell Pug on it.

[Exit.

BRAINSICK
She knows it already, by your favour—

[Knocking.

Sound a retreat, you lusty lovers, or the enemy will charge you in the flank, with a fresh reserve: March off, march off upon the spur, ere he can reach you.

[Enter **WOODALL**.

WOODALL
How now, baron Tell-clock[12], is the passage clear?

BRAINSICK
Clear as a level, without hills or woods, and void of ambuscade.

WOODALL
But Limberham will return immediately, when he finds not his mistress where he thought he left her.

BRAINSICK
Friendship, which has done much, will yet do more.

[Shows a key.]

With this passe par tout, I will instantly conduct her to my own chamber, that she may out-face the keeper, she has been there; and, when my wife returns, who is my slave, I will lay my conjugal commands upon her, to affirm, they have been all this time together.

WOODALL
I shall never make you amends for this kindness, my dear Padron. But would it not be better, if you would take the pains to run after Limberham, and stop him in his way ere he reach the place where he thinks he left his mistress; then hold him in discourse as long as possibly you can, till you guess your wife may be returned, that so they may appear together?

BRAINSICK
I warrant you: laissez faire a Marc Antoine.

[Exit.

WOODALL
Now, madam, you may venture out in safety.

Mrs BRAINSICK [Entering.]
Pray heaven I may.

[Noise.

WOODALL
Hark! I hear Judith's voice: it happens well that she's returned: slip into your chamber immediately, and send back the gown.

Mrs BRAINSICK
I will:—but are not you a wicked man, to put me into all this danger?

[Exit.

WOODALL

Let what can happen, my comfort is, at least, I have enjoyed. But this is no place for consideration. Be jogging, good Mr Woodall, out of this family, while you are well; and go plant in some other country, where your virtues are not so famous.

[Going.

[Enter **Mrs TRICKSY**, with a box of writings.

Mrs TRICKSY

What, wandering up and down, as if you wanted an owner? Do you know that I am lady of the manor; and that all wefts and strays belong to me?

WOODALL

I have waited for you above an hour; but friar Bacon's head has been lately speaking to me,—that time is past. In a word, your keeper has been here, and will return immediately; we must defer our happiness till some more favourable time.

Mrs TRICKSY

I fear him not; he has this morning armed me against himself, by this settlement; the next time he rebels, he gives me a fair occasion of leaving him for ever.

WOODALL

But is this conscience in you? not to let him have his bargain, when he has paid so dear for it?

Mrs TRICKSY

You do not know him: he must perpetually be used ill, or he insults. Besides, I have gained an absolute dominion over him: he must not see, when I bid him wink. If you argue after this, either you love me not, or dare not.

WOODALL

Go in, madam: I was never dared before. I'll but scout a little, and follow you immediately.

[**Mrs TRICKSY** goes in.]

I find a mistress is only kept for other men: and the keeper is but her man in a green livery, bound to serve a warrant for the doe, whenever she pleases, or is in season.

[Enter **JUDITH**, with the Night-gown.

JUDITH

Still you're a lucky man! Mr Brainsick has been exceeding honourable: he ran, as if a legion of bailiffs had been at his heels, and overtook Limberham in the street. Here, take the gown; lay it where you found it, and the danger's over.

WOODALL

Speak softly; Mrs Tricksy is returned.

[Looks in.]

Oh, she's gone into her closet, to lay up her writings: I can throw it on the bed, ere she perceive it has been wanting.

[Throws it in.

JUDITH
Every woman would not have done this for you, which I have done.

WOODALL
I am sensible of it, little Judith; there's a time to come shall pay for all. I hear her returning: not a word; away.

[Exit **JUDITH**.

[Re-enter **Mrs TRICKSY**.

Mrs TRICKSY
What, is a second summons needful? my favours have not been so cheap, that they should stick upon my hands. It seems, you slight your bill of fare, because you know it; or fear to be invited to your loss.

WOODALL
I was willing to secure my happiness from interruption. A true soldier never falls upon the plunder, while the enemy is in the field.

Mrs TRICKSY
He has been so often baffled, that he grows contemptible. Were he here, should he see you enter into my closet; yet—

WOODALL
You are like to be put upon the trial, for I hear his voice.

Mrs TRICKSY
'Tis so: go in, and mark the event now: be but as unconcerned, as you are safe, and trust him to my management.

WOODALL
I must venture it; because to be seen here would have the same effect, as to be taken within. Yet I doubt you are too confident.

[He goes in.

[Enter **LIMBERHAM** and **BRAINSICK**.

LIMBERHAM
How now, Pug? returned so soon!

Mrs TRICKSY

When I saw you came not for me, I was loth to be long without you.

LIMBERHAM

But which way came you, that I saw you not?

Mrs TRICKSY

The back way; by the garden door.

LIMBERHAM

How long have you been here?

Mrs TRICKSY

Just come before you.

LIMBERHAM

O, then all's well. For, to tell you true, Pug, I had a kind of villainous apprehension that you had been here longer: but whatever thou sayest is an oracle, sweet Pug, and I am satisfied.

BRAINSICK [Aside.]

How infinitely she gulls him! and he so stupid not to find it! [To her.] If he be still within, madam, (you know my meaning?) here's Bilbo ready to forbid your keeper entrance.

Mrs TRICKSY [Aside.]

Woodall must have told him of our appointment.—What think you of walking down, Mr Limberham?

LIMBERHAM

I'll but visit the chamber a little first.

Mrs TRICKSY

What new maggot's this? you dare not, sure, be jealous!

LIMBERHAM

No, I protest, sweet Pug, I am not: only to satisfy my curiosity; that's but reasonable, you know.

Mrs TRICKSY

Come, what foolish curiosity?

LIMBERHAM

You must know, Pug, I was going but just now, in obedience to your commands, to enquire of the health and safety of your jewels, and my brother Brainsick most barbarously forbade me entrance:—nay, I dare accuse you, when Pug's by to back me;—but now I am resolved I will go see them, or somebody shall smoke for it.

BRAINSICK

But I resolve you shall not. If she pleases to command my person, I can comply with the obligation of a cavalier.

Mrs TRICKSY
But what reason had you to forbid him, then, sir?

LIMBERHAM
Ay, what reason had you to forbid me, then, sir?

BRAINSICK
'Twas only my caprichio, madam.—Now must I seem ignorant of what she knows full well. [Aside.

Mrs TRICKSY
We'll enquire the cause at better leisure; come down, Mr Limberham.

LIMBERHAM
Nay, if it were only his caprichio, I am satisfied; though I must tell you, I was in a kind of huff, to hear him Tan ta ra, tan ta ra, a quarter of an hour together; for Tan ta ra is but an odd kind of sound, you know, before a man's chamber.

[Enter **PLEASANCE**.

PLEASANCE [Aside.]
Judith has assured me, he must be there; and, I am resolved, I'll satisfy my revenge at any rate upon my rivals.

Mrs TRICKSY
Mrs Pleasance is come to call us: pray let us go.

PLEASANCE
Oh dear, Mr Limberham, I have had the dreadfullest dream to-night, and am come to tell it you: I dreamed you left your mistress's jewels in your chamber, and the door open.

LIMBERHAM
In good time be it spoken; and so I did, Mrs Pleasance.

PLEASANCE
And that a great swinging thief came in, and whipt them out.

LIMBERHAM
Marry, heaven forbid!

Mrs TRICKSY
This is ridiculous: I'll speak to your mother, madam, not to suffer you to eat such heavy suppers.

LIMBERHAM
Nay, that's very true; for, you may remember she fed very much upon larks and pigeons; and they are very heavy meat, as Pug says.

Mrs TRICKSY
The jewels are all safe; I looked on them.

BRAINSICK

Will you never stand corrected, Mrs Pleasance?

PLEASANCE

Not by you; correct your matrimony.—And methought, of a sudden this thief was turned to Mr Woodall; and that, hearing Mr Limberham come, he slipt for fear into the closet.

Mrs TRICKSY

I looked all over it; I'm sure he is not there.—Come away, dear.

BRAINSICK

What, I think you are in a dream too, brother Limberham.

LIMBERHAM

If her dream should come out now! 'tis good to be sure, however.

Mrs TRICKSY

You are sure; have not I said it?—You had best make Mr Woodall a thief, madam.

PLEASANCE

I make him nothing, madam: but the thief in my dream was like Mr Woodall; and that thief may have made Mr Limberham something.

LIMBERHAM

Nay, Mr Woodall is no thief, that's certain; but if a thief should be turned to Mr Woodall, that may be something.

Mrs TRICKSY

Then I'll fetch out the jewels: will that satisfy you?

BRAINSICK

That shall satisfy him.

LIMBERHAM

Yes, that shall satisfy me.

PLEASANCE

Then you are a predestinated fool, and somewhat worse, that shall be nameless. Do you not see how grossly she abuses you? my life on't, there's somebody within, and she knows it; otherwise she would suffer you to bring out the jewels.

LIMBERHAM

Nay, I am no predestinated fool; and therefore, Pug, give way.

Mrs TRICKSY

I will not satisfy your humour.

LIMBERHAM

Then I will satisfy it myself: for my generous blood is up, and I'll force my entrance.

BRAINSICK

Here's Bilbo, then, shall bar you; atoms are not so small, as I will slice the slave. Ha! fate and furies!

LIMBERHAM

Ay, for all your fate and furies, I charge you, in his majesty's name, to keep the peace: now, disobey authority, if you dare.

Mrs TRICKSY

Fear him not, sweet Mr Brainsick.

PLEASANCE [to **BRAINSICK**]

But, if you should hinder him, he may trouble you at law, sir, and say you robbed him of his jewels.

LIMBERHAM

That is well thought on. I will accuse him heinously; there—and therefore fear and tremble.

BRAINSICK

My allegiance charms me: I acquiesce. The occasion is plausible to let him pass.—Now let the burnished beams upon his brow blaze broad, for the brand he cast upon the Brainsick.   [Aside.

Mrs TRICKSY

Dear Mr Limberham, come back, and hear me.

LIMBERHAM

Yes, I will hear thee, Pug.

PLEASANCE

Go on; my life for yours, he is there.

LIMBERHAM

I am deaf as an adder; I will not hear thee, nor have no commiseration.

[Struggles from her, and rushes in.

Mrs TRICKSY

Then I know the worst, and care not.

[**LIMBERHAM** comes running out with the Jewels, followed by **WOODALL**, with his Sword drawn.

LIMBERHAM

O save me, Pug, save me!

[Gets behind her.

WOODALL

A slave, to come and interrupt me at my devotions! but I will—

LIMBERHAM
Hold, hold, since you are so devout; for heaven's sake, hold!

BRAINSICK
Nay, monsieur Woodall!

Mrs TRICKSY
For my sake, spare him.

LIMBERHAM
Yes, for Pug's sake, spare me.

WOODALL
I did his chamber the honour, when my own was not open, to retire thither; and he to disturb me, like a profane rascal as he was.

LIMBERHAM [Aside.]
I believe he had the devil for his chaplain, an' a man durst tell him so.

WOODALL
What is that you mutter?

LIMBERHAM
Nay, nothing; but that I thought you had not been so well given. I was only afraid of Pug's jewels.

WOODALL
What, does he take me for a thief? nay then—

LIMBERHAM
O mercy, mercy!

PLEASANCE
Hold, sir; it was a foolish dream of mine that set him on. I dreamt, a thief, who had been just reprieved for a former robbery, was venturing his neck a minute after in Mr Limberham's closet.

WOODALL
Are you thereabouts, i'faith! A pox of Artemidorus[13].

Mrs TRICKSY
I have had a dream, too, concerning Mrs Brainsick, and perhaps—

WOODALL
Mrs Tricksy, a word in private with you, by your keeper's leave.

LIMBERHAM

Yes, sir, you may speak your pleasure to her; and, if you have a mind to go to prayers together, the closet is open.

WOODALL [To **Mrs TRICKSY**]

You but suspect it at most, and cannot prove it: if you value me, you will not engage me in a quarrel with her husband.

Mrs TRICKSY

Well, in hope you will love me, I will obey.

BRAINSICK

Now, damsel Tricksy, your dream, your dream!

Mrs TRICKSY

It was something of a flagelet, that a shepherd played upon so sweetly, that three women followed him for his music, and still one of them snatched it from the other.

PLEASANCE [Aside.]

I understand her; but I find she is bribed to secrecy.

LIMBERHAM

That flagelet was, by interpretation,—but let that pass; and Mr Woodall, there, was the shepherd, that played the tan ta ra upon it: but a generous heart, like mine, will endure the infamy no longer; therefore, Pug, I banish thee for ever.

Mrs TRICKSY

Then farewell.

LIMBERHAM

Is that all you make of me?

Mrs TRICKSY

I hate to be tormented with your jealous humours, and am glad to be rid of them.

LIMBERHAM

Bear witness, good people, of her ingratitude! Nothing vexes me, but that she calls me jealous; when I found him as close as a butterfly in her closet.

Mrs TRICKSY

No matter for that; I knew not he was there.

LIMBERHAM

Would I could believe thee!

WOODALL

You have both our words for it.

Mrs TRICKSY

Why should you persuade him against his will?

LIMBERHAM
Since you won't persuade me, I care not much; here are the jewels in my possession, and I'll fetch out the settlement immediately.

WOODALL [Shewing the Box.]
Look you, sir, I'll spare your pains; four hundred a-year will serve to comfort a poor cast mistress.

LIMBERHAM
I thought what would come of your devil's pater nosters!

BRAINSICK
Restore it to him for pity, Woodall.

Mrs TRICKSY
I make him my trustee; he shall not restore it.

LIMBERHAM
Here are jewels, that cost me above two thousand pounds; a queen might wear them. Behold this orient necklace, Pug! 'tis pity any neck should touch it, after thine, that pretty neck! but oh, 'tis the falsest neck that e'er was hanged in pearl.

WOODALL
'Twould become your bounty to give it her at parting.

LIMBERHAM
Never the sooner for your asking. But oh, that word parting! can I bear it? if she could find in her heart but so much grace, as to acknowledge what a traitress she has been, I think, in my conscience I could forgive her.

Mrs TRICKSY
I'll not wrong my innocence so much, nor this gentleman's; but, since you have accused us falsely, four hundred a-year betwixt us two will make us some part of reparation.

WOODALL
I answer you not, but with my leg, madam.

PLEASANCE [Aside.]
This mads me; but I cannot help it.

LIMBERHAM
What, wilt thou kill me, Pug, with thy unkindness, when thou knowest I cannot live without thee? It goes to my heart, that this wicked fellow—

WOODALL
How's that, sir?

LIMBERHAM
Under the rose, good Mr Woodall; but, I speak it with all submission, in the bitterness of my spirit, that you, or any man, should have the disposing of my four hundred a-year gratis; therefore dear Pug, a word in private, with your permission, good Mr Woodall.

Mrs TRICKSY
Alas, I know, by experience, I may safely trust my person with you.

[Exeunt **LIMBERHAM** and **TRICKSY**.

[Enter **ALDO**.

PLEASANCE
O, father Aldo, we have wanted you! Here has been made the rarest discovery!

BRAINSICK
With the most comical catastrophe!

WOODALL
Happily arrived, i'faith, my old sub-fornicator; I have been taken up on suspicion here with Mrs Tricksy.

ALDO
To be taken, to be seen! Before George, that's a point next the worst, son Woodall.

WOODALL
Truth is, I wanted thy assistance, old Methusalem; but, my comfort is, I fell greatly.

ALDO
Well, young Phæton, that's somewhat yet, if you made a blaze at your departure.

[Enter **GILES, Mrs BRAINSICK,** and **JUDITH**.

GILES
By your leave, gentlemen, I have followed an old master of mine these two long hours, and had a fair course at him up the street; here he entered, I'm sure.

ALDO
Whoop holyday! our trusty and well-beloved Giles, most welcome! Now for some news of my ungracious son.

WOODALL [Aside.]
Giles here! O rogue, rogue! Now, would I were safe stowed over head and ears in the chest again.

ALDO
Look you now, son Woodall, I told you I was not mistaken; my rascal's in town, with a vengeance to him.

GILES
Why, this is he, sir; I thought you had known him.

ALDO
Known whom?

GILES
Your son here, my young master.

ALDO
Do I dote? or art thou drunk, Giles?

GILES
Nay, I am sober enough, I'm sure; I have been kept fasting almost these two days.

ALDO
Before George, 'tis so! I read it in that leering look: What a Tartar have I caught!

BRAINSICK
Woodall his son!

PLEASANCE
What, young father Aldo!

ALDO [Aside.]
Now cannot I for shame hold up my head, to think what this young rogue is privy to!

Mrs BRAINSICK
The most dumb interview I ever saw!

BRAINSICK
What, have you beheld the Gorgon's head on either side?

ALDO
Oh, my sins! my sins! and he keeps my book of conscience too! He can display them, with a witness! Oh, treacherous young devil!

WOODALL [Aside.]
Well, the squib's run to the end of the line, and now for the cracker: I must bear up.

ALDO
I must set a face of authority on the matter, for my credit.—Pray, who am I? do you know me, sir?

WOODALL
Yes, I think I should partly know you, sir: You may remember some private passages betwixt us.

ALDO [Aside.]
I thought as much; he has me already!—But pray, sir, why this ceremony amongst friends? Put on, put on; and let us hear what news from France. Have you heard lately from my son? does he continue still

the most hopeful and esteemed young gentleman in Paris? does he manage his allowance with the same discretion? and, lastly, has he still the same respect and duty for his good old father?

WOODALL
Faith, sir, I have been too long from my catechism, to answer so many questions; but, suppose there be no news of your quondam son, you may comfort up your heart for such a loss; father Aldo has a numerous progeny about the town, heaven bless them.

ALDO
It is very well, sir; I find you have been searching for your relations, then, in Whetstone's Park[14]!

WOODALL
No, sir; I made some scruple of going to the foresaid place, for fear of meeting my own father there.

ALDO
Before George, I could find in my heart to disinherit thee.

PLEASANCE
Sure you cannot be so unnatural.

WOODALL
I am sure I am no bastard; witness one good quality I have. If any of your children have a stronger tang of the father in them, I am content to be disowned.

ALDO
Well, from this time forward, I pronounce thee—no son of mine.

WOODALL
Then you desire I should proceed to justify I am lawfully begotten? The evidence is ready, sir; and, if you please, I shall relate, before this honourable assembly, those excellent lessons of morality you gave me at our first acquaintance. As, in the first place—

ALDO
Hold, hold; I charge thee hold, on thy obedience. I forgive thee heartily: I have proof enough thou art my son; but tame thee that can, thou art a mad one.

PLEASANCE
Why this is as it should be.

ALDO [To him.]
Not a word of any passages betwixt us; it is enough we know each other; hereafter we will banish all pomp and ceremony, and live familiarly together. I'll be Pylades, and thou mad Orestes, and we will divide the estate betwixt us, and have fresh wenches, and ballum rankum every night.

WOODALL
A match, i'faith: and let the world pass.

ALDO

But hold a little; I had forgot one point: I hope you are not married, nor engaged?

WOODALL
To nothing but my pleasures, I.

ALDO
A mingle of profit would do well though. Come, here is a girl; look well upon her; it is a mettled toad, I can tell you that: She will make notable work betwixt two sheets, in a lawful way.

WOODALL
What, my old enemy, Mrs Pleasance!

Mrs BRAINSICK
Marry Mrs Saintly's daughter!

ALDO
The truth is, she has past for her daughter, by my appointment; but she has as good blood running in her veins, as the best of you. Her father, Mr Palms, on his death-bed, left her to my care and disposal, besides a fortune of twelve hundred a year; a pretty convenience, by my faith.

WOODALL
Beyond my hopes, if she consent.

ALDO
I have taken some care of her education, and placed her here with Mrs Saintly, as her daughter, to avoid her being blown upon by fops, and younger brothers. So now, son, I hope I have matched your concealment with my discovery; there is hit for hit, ere I cross the cudgels.

PLEASANCE
You will not take them up, sir?

WOODALL
I dare not against you, madam: I am sure you will worst me at all weapons. All I can say is, I do not now begin to love you.

ALDO
Let me speak for thee: Thou shalt be used, little Pleasance, like a sovereign princess: Thou shalt not touch a bit of butchers' meat in a twelve-month; and thou shall be treated—

PLEASANCE
Not with ballum rankum every night, I hope!

ALDO
Well, thou art a wag; no more of that. Thou shall want neither man's meat, nor woman's meat, as far as his provision will hold out.

PLEASANCE

But I fear he is so horribly given to go a house-warming abroad, that the least part of the provision will come to my share at home.

WOODALL
You will find me so much employment in my own family, that I shall have little need to look out for journey-work.

ALDO
Before George, he shall do thee reason, ere thou sleepest.

PLEASANCE
No; he shall have an honourable truce for one day at least; for it is not fair to put a fresh enemy upon him.

Mrs BRAINSICK [To **PLEASANCE**]
I beseech you, madam, discover nothing betwixt him and me.

PLEASANCE [To her.]
I am contented to cancel the old score; but take heed of bringing me an after-reckoning.

[Enter **GERVASE**, leading **Mrs SAINTLY**.

GERVASE
Save you, gentlemen; and you, my quondam master: You are welcome all, as I may say.

ALDO
How now, sirrah? what is the matter?

GERVASE
Give good words, while you live, sir; your landlord, and Mr Saintly, if you please.

WOODALL
Oh, I understand the business; he is married to the widow.

Mrs SAINTLY
Verily the good work is accomplished.

BRAINSICK
But, why Mr Saintly?

GERVASE
When a man is married to his betters, it is but decency to take her name. A pretty house, a pretty situation, and prettily furnished! I have been unlawfully labouring at hard duty; but a parson has soldered up the matter: Thank your worship, Mr Woodall—How? Giles here!

WOODALL
This business is out, and I am now Aldo. My father has forgiven me, and we are friends.

GERVASE

When will Giles, with his honesty, come to this?

WOODALL

Nay, do not insult too much, good Mr Saintly: Thou wert but my deputy; thou knowest the widow intended it to me.

GERVASE

But I am satisfied she performed it with me, sir. Well, there is much good will in these precise old women; they are the most zealous bed-fellows! Look, an' she does not blush now! you see there is grace in her.

WOODALL

Mr Limberham, where are you? Come, cheer up, man! How go matters on your side of the country? Cry him, Gervase.

GERVASE

Mr Limberham, Mr Limberham, make your appearance in the court, and save your recognizance.

[Enter **LIMBERHAM** and **Mrs TRICKSY**.

WOODALL

Sir, I should now make a speech to you in my own defence; but the short of all is this: If you can forgive what is past, your hand, and I'll endeavour to make up the breach betwixt you and your mistress: If not, I am ready to give you the satisfaction of a gentleman.

LIMBERHAM

Sir, I am a peaceable man, and a good Christian, though I say it, and desire no satisfaction from any man. Pug and I are partly agreed upon the point already; and therefore lay thy hand upon thy heart, Pug, and, if thou canst, from the bottom of thy soul, defy mankind, naming no body, I'll forgive thy past enormities; and, to give good example to all Christian keepers, will take thee to be my wedded wife; and thy four hundred a-year shall be settled upon thee, for separate maintenance.

Mrs TRICKSY

Why, now I can consent with honour.

ALDO

This is the first business that was ever made up without me.

WOODALL

Give you joy, Mr Bridegroom.

LIMBERHAM

You may spare your breath, sir, if you please; I desire none from you. It is true, I am satisfied of her virtue, in spite of slander; but, to silence calumny, I shall civilly desire you henceforth, not to make a chapel-of-ease of Pug's closet.

PLEASANCE [Aside.]

I'll take care of false worship, I'll warrant him.
He shall have no more to do with Bel and the Dragon.

BRAINSICK
Come hither, wedlock, and let me seal my lasting love upon thy lips. Saintly has been seduced, and so has Tricksy; but thou alone art kind and constant. Hitherto I have not valued modesty, according to its merit; but hereafter, Memphis shall not boast a monument more firm than my affection.

WOODALL
A most excellent reformation, and at a most seasonable time! The moral of it is pleasant, if well considered. Now, let us to dinner.—Mrs Saintly, lead the way, as becomes you, in your own house.

[The rest going off.

PLEASANCE
Your hand, sweet moiety.

WOODALL
And heart too, my comfortable importance.
Mistress and wife, by turns, I have possessed:
He, who enjoys them both in one, is blessed.

Footnotes
1. The Mahommedan doctrine of predestination is well known. They reconcile themselves to all dispensations, by saying, "They are written on the forehead" of him, to whose lot they have fallen.

2. The custom of drinking supernaculum, consisted in turning down the cup upon the thumb-nail of the drinker after his pledge, when, if duly quaffed off, no drop of liquor ought to appear upon his nail.

With that she set it to her nose,
And off at once the rumkin goes;
No drops beside her muzzle falling,
Until that she had supped it all in:
Then turning't topsey on her thumb,
Says—look, here's supernaculum.
Cotton's Virgil travestie.

This custom seems to have been derived from the Germans, who held, that if a drop appeared on the thumb, it presaged grief and misfortune to the person whose health was drunk.

3. This piece of dirty gallantry seems to have been fashionable:

Come, Phyllis, thy finger, to begin the go round;
How the glass in thy hand with charms does abound!
You and the wine to each other lend arms,
And I find that my love
Does for either improve,

For that does redouble, as you double your charms.

4. Dapper, a silly character in Jonson's Alchemist, tricked by an astrologer, who persuades him the queen of fairies is his aunt.

5. The mask, introduced in the first act of the Maid's Tragedy, ends with the following dialogue betwixt Cinthia and Night:

Cinthia Whip up thy team,
The day breaks here, and yon sun-flaring beam
Shot from the south. Say, which way wilt thou go?

Night. I'll vanish into mists.

Cinthia. I into day.

6. In spring 1677, whilst the treaty of Nimeguen was under discussion, the French took the three important frontier towns, Valenciennes, St Omer, and Cambray. The Spaniards seemed, with the most passive infatuation, to have left the defence of Flanders to the Prince of Orange and the Dutch.

7. Alluding to the imaginary history of Pine, a merchant's clerk, who, being wrecked on a desert island in the South Seas, bestowed on it his own name, and peopled it by the assistance of his master's daughter and her two maid servants, who had escaped from the wreck by his aid.

8. Sulli, the famous composer.

9. It would seem that about this time the French were adopting their present mode of pronunciation, so capriciously distinct from the orthography.

10. "Queen Dido, or the wandering Prince of Troy," an old ballad, printed in the "Reliques of Ancient Poetry," in which the ghost of queen Dido thus addresses the perfidious Æneas:

Therefore prepare thy flitting soul,
To wander with me in the air;
When deadly grief shall make it howl,
Because of me thou took'st no care.
Delay not time, thy glass is run,
Thy date is past, thy life is done.

11. Pricking, in hare-hunting, is tracking the foot of the game by the eye, when the scent is lost.]

12. The facetious Tom Brown, in his 2d dialogue on Mr Bayes' changing his religion, introduces our poet saying,

"Likewise he (Cleveland) having the misfortune to call that domestic animal a cock,

The Baron Tell-clock of the night,

I could never, igad, as I came home from the tavern, meet a watchman or so, but I presently asked him, 'Baron Tell-clock of the night, pr'ythee how goes the time?"

13. Artemidorus, the sophist of Cnidos, was the soothsayer who prophesied the death of Cæsar. Shakespeare has introduced him in his tragedy of "Julius Cæsar."

14. A common rendezvous of the rakes and bullies of the time; "For when they expected the most polished hero in Nemours, I gave them a ruffian reeking from Whetstone's Park." Dedication to Lee's "Princess of Cleves." In his translation of Ovid's "Love Elegies," Lib. II, Eleg. XIX. Dryden mentions, "an easy Whetstone whore."

EPILOGUE

SPOKEN BY LIMBERHAM.

I beg a boon, that, ere you all disband,
Some one would take my bargain off my hand:
To keep a punk is but a common evil;
To find her false, and marry,—that's the devil.
Well, I ne'er acted part in all my life,
But still I was fobbed off with some such wife.
I find the trick; these poets take no pity
Of one that is a member of the city.
We cheat you lawfully, and in our trades;
You cheat us basely with your common jades.
Now I am married, I must sit down by it;
But let me keep my dear-bought spouse in quiet.
Let none of you damned Woodalls of the pit,
Put in for shares to mend our breed in wit;
We know your bastards from our flesh and blood,
Not one in ten of yours e'er comes to good.
In all the boys, their fathers' virtues shine,
But all the female fry turn Pugs—like mine.
When these grow up, Lord, with what rampant gadders
Our counters will be thronged, and roads with padders!
This town two bargains has, not worth one farthing,—
A Smithfield horse, and wife of Covent-Garden[1].

Footnote

1. Alluding to an old proverb, that whoso goes to Westminster for a wife, to St Paul's for a man, and to Smithfield for a horse, may meet with a whore, a knave, and a jade. Falstaff, on being informed that Bardolph is gone to Smithfield to buy him a horse, observes, "I bought him in Paul's, and he'll buy me a

horse in Smithfield; an I could get me but a wife in the stews, I were manned, horsed, and wived." Second Part of Henry IV. Act I. Scene II.

John Dryden – A Short Biography

John Dryden was born on August 9th, 1631 in the village rectory of Aldwincle near Thrapston in Northamptonshire, where his maternal grandfather was Rector of All Saints Church.

Dryden was the eldest of fourteen children born to Erasmus Dryden and wife Mary Pickering, paternal grandson of Sir Erasmus Dryden, 1st Baronet (1553–1632) and wife Frances Wilkes, Puritan landowning gentry who supported the Puritan cause and Parliament.

As a boy Dryden lived in the nearby village of Titchmarsh, Northamptonshire where it is probable that he received his first education.

In 1644 he was sent to Westminster School as a King's Scholar where his headmaster was Dr. Richard Busby, a charismatic teacher but severe disciplinarian. Having recently been re-founded by Elizabeth I, Westminster now embraced a very different religious and political spirit encouraging royalism and high Anglicanism but as a humanist public school, it maintained a curriculum which trained pupils in the art of rhetoric and the presentation of arguments for both sides of a given issue. This skill would remain with Dryden and influence his later writing and thinking, as much of it displays these dialectical patterns.

His first published poem, whilst still at Westminster, was an elegy with a strong royalist flavour on the death of his schoolmate Henry, Lord Hastings from smallpox, and alludes to the execution of King Charles I, which took place on January 30th, 1649.

In 1650 Dryden was ready for University and travelled to Trinity College, Cambridge. Dryden's undergraduate years would almost certainly have followed the standard curriculum of classics, rhetoric, and mathematics.

Dryden obtained his BA in 1654, graduating top of the list for Trinity that year.

However family tragedy struck in June of the same year when Dryden's father died, leaving him some land which generated a small income, but not enough to live on.

Returning to London during The Protectorate, Dryden now obtained work with Cromwell's Secretary of State, John Thurloe. This may have been the result of influence exercised on his behalf by his cousin the Lord Chamberlain, Sir Gilbert Pickering.

At Cromwell's funeral on 23 November 1658 Dryden was in the company of the Puritan poets John Milton and Andrew Marvell. The setting was to be a sea change in English history. From Republic to Monarchy and from one set of lauded poets to what would soon become the Age of Dryden.

The start began later that year when Dryden published the first of his great poems, Heroic Stanzas (1658), a eulogy on Cromwell's death which is necessarily cautious and prudent in its emotional display.

With the Restoration of the Monarchy in 1660 Dryden celebrated in verse with Astraea Redux, an authentic royalist panegyric. In this work the interregnum is illustrated as a time of anarchy, and Charles is seen as the restorer of peace and order.

With the king now established Dryden moved quickly to place himself as the leading poet and critic of his day and transferred his allegiances to the new government.

Along with Astraea Redux, Dryden welcomed the new regime with two more panegyrics: To His Sacred Majesty: A Panegyric on his Coronation (1662) and To My Lord Chancellor (1662).

These panegyrics are occasional and written to celebrate events. Thus they are written for the nation rather than the self, but these and others put him in good standing for his eventual appointment as Poet Laureate, where a number of event poems would be required each year and speaking for the Nation and to the Nation would be the first order of duty.

These poems suggest that Dryden was looking to court a possible patron which would have given him an income and time to explore his creative ideas but no, his path instead would be to make a living in writing for publishers, not for the aristocracy, and thus ultimately for the reading public.

In November 1662 Dryden was proposed for membership in the Royal Society, and he was elected an early fellow. However, his inactivity and non payment of dues led to his expulsion in 1666.

On December 1st, 1663 Dryden married the Royalist sister of Sir Robert Howard—Lady Elizabeth Howard (died 1714). The marriage was at St. Swithin's, London, and the consent of the parents is noted on the license, though Lady Elizabeth was then about twenty-five. She was the object of some scandals, well or ill founded; it was said that Dryden had been bullied into the marriage by her brothers. A small estate in Wiltshire was settled upon them by her father. The lady's intellect and temper were apparently not good; her husband was treated as an inferior by those of her social status.

Dryden's works occasionally contain outbursts against the married state but also celebrations of the same. Little else is known of the intimate side of his marriage.

Both Dryden and his wife were warmly attached to their children. They had three sons: Charles (1666–1704), John (1668–1701), and Erasmus Henry (1669–1710). Lady Elizabeth Dryden survived her husband, but went insane soon after his death and died in 1714.

With the re-opening of the theatres after the Puritan ban, Dryden began to also write plays. His first play, The Wild Gallant, appeared in 1663 but was not successful. From 1668 on he was contracted to produce three plays a year for the King's Company, in which he became a shareholder. During the 1660s and '70s, theatrical writing was his main source of income. He led the way in Restoration comedy, his best-known works being Marriage à la Mode (1672), as well as heroic tragedy and regular tragedy, in which his greatest success was All for Love (1678). Dryden was never fully satisfied with his theatrical writings and frequently suggested that his talents were wasted on unworthy audiences.

Certainly therefore fame as a poet looked more rewarding. In 1667, around the same time his dramatic career began, he published Annus Mirabilis, a lengthy historical poem which described the English defeat of the Dutch naval fleet and the Great Fire of London in 1666. It was a modern epic in pentameter quatrains that established him as the pre-eminent poet of his generation, and was crucial in his attaining the posts of Poet Laureate (1668) and then historiographer royal (1670).

When the Great Plague of London closed the theatres in 1665 Dryden retreated to Wiltshire where he wrote Of Dramatick Poesie (1668), arguably the best of his unsystematic prefaces and essays. Dryden constantly defended his own literary practice, and Of Dramatick Poesie, the longest of his critical works, takes the form of a dialogue in which four characters—each based on a prominent contemporary, with Dryden himself as 'Neander'—debate the merits of classical, French and English drama.

He felt strongly about the relation of the poet to tradition and the creative process, and his heroic play Aureng-zebe (1675) has a prologue which denounces the use of rhyme in serious drama. His play All for Love (1678) was written in blank verse, and was to immediately follow Aureng-Zebe.

On December 18th, 1679 he was attacked in Rose Alley near his home in Covent Garden by thugs hired by fellow poet, John Wilmot, 2nd Earl of Rochester, with whom he had a long-standing conflict. Wilmot was constantly in and out of favour with the King and his own poetry was often bawdy, lewd, even obscene and made fun of the King who would often exile him from Court.

Dryden's greatest achievements were in satiric verse: the mock-heroic Mac Flecknoe, a more personal product of his Laureate years, was a lampoon circulated in manuscript and an attack on the playwright Thomas Shadwell. Dryden's main goal in the work is to "satirize Shadwell, ostensibly for his offenses against literature but more immediately we may suppose for his habitual badgering of him on the stage and in print." It is not a belittling form of satire, but rather one which makes his object great in ways which are unexpected, transferring the ridiculous into poetry. This line of satire continued with Absalom and Achitophel (1681) and The Medal (1682). Other major works from this period are the religious poems Religio Laici (1682), written from the position of a member of the Church of England; his 1683 edition of Plutarch's Lives, translated From the Greek by Several Hands in which he introduced the word biography to English readers; and The Hind and the Panther, (1687) which celebrates his conversion to Roman Catholicism.

He wrote Britannia Rediviva celebrating the birth of a son and heir to the Catholic King and Queen on June 10th, 1688. When later in the same year James II was deposed in the Glorious Revolution, Dryden's refusal to take the oaths of allegiance to the new monarchs, William and Mary, which left him out of favour at court and he had to leave his post as Poet Laureate. Thomas Shadwell, his despised rival, succeeded him. Dryden, England's greatest literary figure, was now forced to give up his public offices and live by the proceeds of his pen alone.

Dryden was an excellent translator with his own style which brought the ire of many critics. Many felt he would embellish or expand anything he felt short or curt. Dryden did not feel such expansion was a fault, arguing that as Latin is a naturally concise language it cannot be duly represented by a comparable number of words in the much larger English vocabulary. He continued with his task of translating works by Horace, Juvenal, Ovid, Lucretius, and Theocritus, a task which he found far more satisfying than writing for the stage.

In 1694 he began work on what would be his most ambitious and defining work as translator, The Works of Virgil (1697), which was published by subscription. The publication of the translation of Virgil was a national event and brought Dryden the sum of £1,400.

His final translations appeared in the volume Fables Ancient and Modern (1700), a series of episodes from Homer, Ovid, and Boccaccio, as well as modernised adaptations from Geoffrey Chaucer interspersed with Dryden's own poems. As a translator, he made great literary works in the older languages available to readers of English.

John Dryden died on May 12th, 1700, and was initially buried in St. Anne's cemetery in Soho, before being exhumed and reburied in Westminster Abbey ten days later. He was the subject of poetic eulogies, such as Luctus Brittannici: or the Tears of the British Muses; for the Death of John Dryden, Esq. (London, 1700), and The Nine Muses.

He is seen as dominating the literary life of Restoration England to such a point that the period came to be known in literary circles as the Age of Dryden. Walter Scott called him "Glorious John."

Dryden was the dominant literary figure and influence of his age. He established the heroic couplet as a standard form of English poetry by writing successful satires, religious pieces, fables, epigrams, compliments, prologues, and plays with it; he also introduced the alexandrine and triplet into the form. In his poems, translations, and criticism, he established a poetic diction appropriate to the heroic couplet—Auden referred to him as "the master of the middle style"—that was a model for his contemporaries and for much of the 18th century. The considerable loss felt by the English literary community at his death was evident in the elegies written about him. Dryden's heroic couplet went on to become the dominant poetic form of the 18th century.

What Dryden achieved in his poetry was neither the emotional excitement of the early nineteenth-century romantics nor the intellectual complexities of the metaphysicals. Although he uses formal structures such as heroic couplets, he tried to recreate the natural rhythm of speech, and he knew that different subjects need different kinds of verse. In his preface to Religio Laici he says that "the expressions of a poem designed purely for instruction ought to be plain and natural, yet majestic... The florid, elevated and figurative way is for the passions; for (these) are begotten in the soul by showing the objects out of their true proportion.... A man is to be cheated into passion, but to be reasoned into truth."

Perhaps the following illustrates Dryden and his life—"The way I have taken, is not so streight as Metaphrase, nor so loose as Paraphrase: Some things too I have omitted, and sometimes added of my own. Yet the omissions I hope, are but of Circumstances, and such as wou'd have no grace in English; and the Addition, I also hope, are easily deduc'd from Virgil's Sense. They will seem (at least I have the Vanity to think so), not struck into him, but growing out of him".

John Dryden – A Concise Bibliography

Astraea Redux, 1660
The Wild Gallant (comedy), 1663
The Indian Emperour (tragedy), 1665
Annus Mirabilis (poem), 1667
The Enchanted Island (comedy), 1667, with William D'Avenant from Shakespeare's The Tempest
Secret Love, or The Maiden Queen, 1667
An Essay of Dramatick Poesie, 1668

An Evening's Love (comedy), 1668
Tyrannick Love (tragedy), 1669
The Conquest of Granada, 1670
The Assignation, or Love in a Nunnery, 1672
Marriage à la mode, 1672
Amboyna, or the Cruelties of the Dutch to the English Merchants, 1673
The Mistaken Husband (comedy), 1674
Aureng-zebe, 1675
All for Love, 1678
Oedipus (heroic drama), 1679, an adaptation with Nathaniel Lee of Sophocles' Oedipus
Absalom and Achitophel, 1681
The Spanish Fryar, 1681
Mac Flecknoe, 1682
The Medal, 1682
Religio Laici, 1682
To the Memory of Mr. Oldham, 1684
Threnodia Augustalis, 1685
The Hind and the Panther, 1687
A Song for St. Cecilia's Day, 1687
Britannia Rediviva, 1688, written to mark the birth of a Prince of Wales.
Amphitryon, 1690
Don Sebastian (play), 1690
Creator Spirit, by whose aid, 1690. Translation of Rabanus Maurus' Veni Creator Spiritus
King Arthur, 1691
Cleomenes, 1692
The Art of Satire, 1693
Love Triumphant, 1694
The Works of Virgil, 1697
Alexander's Feast, 1697
Fables, Ancient and Modern, 1700

Printed in Great Britain
by Amazon